*Sunset* **BATHROOMS**
planning &
remodeling

SUNSET BOOKS ■ MENLO PARK, CALIFORNIA

# Sunset

## SUNSET BOOKS

Vice President, General Manager: Richard A. Smeby
Editorial Director: Bob Doyle
Production Director: Lory Day
Art Director: Vasken Guiragossian

**Staff for this edition:**
Developmental Editor: Jeff Beneke
Editor: Linda Hetzer
Consultant: Ed Lipinski
Art Direction: Richard J. Berenson,
          Berenson Design & Books, Ltd.
Computer Production: Robert Steimle
Revised Illustrations: Ed Lam
Photo Research: Ede Rothaus
Assistant Editor: John Glenn
Editorial Assistants: Erica Toth, Carrie Glidden
Production Assistant: Patricia S. Williams
Cover Design: Vasken Guiragossian

## BATHROOMS: PLANNING & REMODELING

was produced in conjunction with Roundtable Press, Inc.
Directors: Marsha Melnick, Susan E. Meyer, Julie Merberg

First printing, seventh edition

10 9 8 7 6 5 4 3 2
Copyright © 2000, 1994, 1983, 1980, 1975,
          1969, 1963
Sunset Publishing Corporation,
Menlo Park, CA 94025.

ISBN 0-376-01329-X
Library of Congress Catalog Card Number: 99-66305

Printed in the United States.

For additional copies of
*Bathrooms: Planning & Remodeling*
or any other Sunset book, call 1-800-526-5111.
Or see our Web site at: www.sunsetbooks.com

# Contents

## A new bathroom

Bathrooms are no longer just utilitarian rooms best kept out of sight. Through a combination of style, craftsmanship, and great fixtures, bathrooms have become attractive and personal oases.

A look through these pages points out the many choices available today. Pedestal sinks, whirlpool bathtubs, steam showers, a variety of surfaces for countertops, and lots of storage units help make a bathroom look great and work even better. This book, which includes design ideas, suggestions for efficient layouts, construction techniques, and a look at a variety of products, presents a review of the entire process from the initial planning phase through the final design to the actual remodeling.

Whether you are hiring a professional or doing the work yourself, this book will help you create a bathroom that is just right for your needs.

# DESIGN IDEAS

The bathroom is no longer the most standardized room in the house. It has developed its own personality. Basic or elegant, modern or traditional, it should be warm enough to invite you to primp but simple enough to get you out quickly. To make your bathroom as individual as you are, it helps to have both information and inspiration. So this chapter is full of color photographs showing bathroom design ideas you can apply to your home, whether you're remodeling or doing a complete renovation.

"Classic layouts" (pages 6–11) shows bathrooms that are small and basic, bathrooms that are luxurious spas, and bathrooms that are any variation in between. "Washing up" (pages 12–17) is what the bathroom is all about, so these pages present the bathroom's basic elements—the sink, the bathtub, and the shower.

Bathroom style is due in part to the choice of materials for the walls, floor, vanity, and storage cabinets. "Surface splendor" (pages 18–21) illustrates a wealth of materials and attractive ways to include them. Proper lighting is essential to good grooming and "Abundant light" (pages 22–25) shows how to make the most of natural light and to capitalize on it with the magic of mirrors.

As we age, our needs change and "Universal design" (pages 26–27) presents the latest views on accessible bathrooms. "A guest's retreat" (pages 28–29) offers ideas for powder rooms or half baths. And, lastly, no bathroom can function properly without good storage. "A place for everything" (pages 30–33) shows clever storage solutions.

**Pale seafoam green** fixtures and bright yellow walls give this bathroom the look of a spring morning. The pedestal sink has a large sculptured bowl that resembles flower petals and the bathtub has a built-in grab bar. The white wall tiles set in a running course and several rows of molding tiles at the top and baseboard enliven this compact room. The molding running just above the window sills emphasizes the large size of the windows and allows the sills to become shelves for toiletries. The stainless steel wastebasket is a nice touch that repeats the color of the chrome-plated fittings and towel bars.

**Tiles in shades of yellow** that cover more than three-quarters of the wall create a sunny backdrop for the freestanding bathtub and low-slung, one-piece toilet. The same tiles are used on the countertop of the clear pine vanity. The thin blue accent line near the top of the tiles calls attention to the height of the tiles and brings into relief the casement window over the toilet. The large blue vase picks up the blue color of the accent tiles, heightening the yellow even more, while the floor tiles in a traditional black and white pattern provide a pleasant counterpoint to the yellow walls.

**A small bathroom takes advantage** of its high ceiling with a majestic arch over the bathtub/shower. The design of the self-rimmed sink is enlarged and repeated in a row of tiles placed at chair-rail height. The geometric design in red with blue and gray accents punctuates the mottled gray wall tiles. The bright red is replicated in the soap dish in the shower and with the towels. The white plastic laminate vanity countertop extends to form a shelf over the toilet. The silver planter and sculpture on the shelf pick up the color of the chrome-plated fittings in the bathtub/shower and the sink.

**Small gray tiles on the walls** and floor create a uniform background for all three areas of this compartmentalized bathroom. Since the only window is in the toilet area, only a partial wall was built so it would not block the light. The shower stall, as seen reflected in the mirror, is next to the toilet and the wall between has towel bars. The main area of the bathroom has two stainless steel sinks placed in a long counter covered with the same small gray tiles. The mirror behind the counter covers the width of the room and extends to the ceiling. The wall sconce (and a matching one not visible) face upward to bounce light off the ceiling. The large mirror reflects this light into the room and increases the sense of space.

**A dramatic color scheme** of black and gold enriches a simple bathroom. The small vanity is black laminate and the sink fittings are gold. The mirror is framed in black and gold. Reflected in the mirror are two prints also with black and gold frames that hang above a striking gold fleur-de-lis towel rack. The shower curtain is black, inset with a decorative gold band. To create the wall treatment, diamond shapes were outlined with masking tape and then every other one was sponged with gold paint. Small stars were then stenciled onto the points of the diamonds.

**Getting away from it all** is very possible in this peaceful bathroom. The upper walls are covered with a pale gold quilted fabric that provides a soft contrast to the stone lower walls. A wide border of mosaic tiles separates the two. The wood parquet floor is a checkerboard pattern of light and dark stained squares. The variety of textures—fabric, stone, mosaic tile, wood—and the rich geometry of the room—the diamonds of the quilted fabric, the small squares of the mosaic tiles, the large rectangles of the stone, and the squares of the checkerboard floor—produce a graphic background for the traditional fixtures, a pedestal sink with its large bowl and thick classical base, and a freestanding bathtub.

**The choice here was to use color** as a means of creating a personality within a very small space. The deep teal blue of the toilet and sink contrasts with the pale marble walls and floor to emphasize the interesting shapes of the fixtures—the funnel-shaped pedestal sink and the low-slung one-piece toilet. The gold fittings and towel bar and gold shower door frame complement the teal blue. The large mirror behind the sink and toilet is trimmed with patterned tiles of copper and gold. The teal light fixtures are attached to this mirror. The entire room with three elements—sink, toilet, and shower stall, all in a row—is reflected in the floor-to-ceiling mirror on the wall to the left.

# Classic layouts

**Soft, warm, and comfortable** describes this bathroom decorated in blue and white, a fresh color combination that's always easy to live with. The large whirlpool tub is set under the triple-pane window, which has a simple sheer white knotted valance because privacy is not an issue on the second floor. The shower stall is large but unobtrusive because the walls are glass. The laminate vanity provides ample storage space. The sprightly blue and white wallpaper picks up the dusty blue carpet and the white of the vanity and stone tub surround.

**Elevated to a new level of luxury,** both literally and figuratively, this bathroom has a splendid view of a city skyline in the distance. The decor of the room is deliberately kept simple to let the view predominate. Gray and white marble tiles cover the walls and floor, and the paneled tub surround is painted in shades of gray and white. The white fixtures have chrome-plated fittings and accessories, and recessed shelves over the bathtub hold toiletries and towels.

**The tranquil look** of this bathroom is a result of both its size and the simplicity of its design. The room was enlarged with a bay window, creating the perfect spot for the whirlpool tub. The shower enclosure with built-in corner shelves is large, but recedes into the background because of its glass walls. The wood vanity has room for two sculptured self-rimmed sinks. Marble tiles in a pale honey color matching the marble vanity countertop cover the walls, floor, and tub surround.

**Master bathrooms are becoming as comfortable** as master bedrooms. Here the peaked ceiling above the window and the steps leading up to it create a thronelike setting for the whirlpool bathtub. The glass shower enclosure is luxurious in size. The marble-topped vanity, with two sinks, sits in front of a bay window topped with a large half-round window. The large windows bring in lots of light. The light colors of the almond laminate vanity, the striated marble floor and tub surround, and the beige walls are accented with gold to give the room a rich look.

# Washing up

**The sculptural wood sink cabinet** and its round mirror on top look almost like an upside-down exclamation point. The doors in the cabinet open to reveal storage. The three different woods used here, the teak sink cabinet, the vanity with a darker wood top, and the tall black lacquer storage cabinet stand out against the all-white walls and floor.

**A Victorian-style mirror** and graceful sconces top a classic pedestal sink with gold fixtures. The flowing lace curtains, the small mahogany end table, and the textured wallpaper complement the pink floral tiles and strengthen the theme of old-world elegance.

**An oversized console sink,** with ample deck space and two thick turned wood legs, has brass fittings. In a simple bathroom with cream walls and white woodwork and very few ornaments, the generous curves and high backsplash of the sink form a focal point.

**A polished marble trough sink** seems like a piece of furniture set against wall and floor tiles in the same color. The sink fittings mounted high on the wall above the sink and a shower area with no door help to focus attention on the sink, whose long expanse of marble provides lots of counter space.

**A new way to present** a sink looks as old as the Tuscan hills. The stone above-the-counter sink sits on a stone slab countertop against a wall of handmade tiles. The mosaic floor and scalloped mirror frame provide softer design notes.

**Two stainless steel sinks** are undermounted in a white marble countertop but sit above a stainless steel counter that tops the blond wood storage cabinet. The industrial look of the sinks is reinforced by the gray metal backsplash, the square faucets and handles, and the double medicine cabinet.

**A sleek pedestal sink** with a large overhanging bowl has sides that extend out to provide space for toiletries and convenient attached towel bars. The gracious front curve of the sink is repeated in the curve of the gooseneck faucet and echoed in the curlicues painted on the mirror frame.

**This generous enclosure** for a tub is the essence of simplicity. Made of wood wainscoting painted white and topped with a cherry wood counter that has a beautiful beveled edge, it gives the tub great presence. White walls and woodwork and matchstick blinds repeat the color scheme of the tub surround. With the two windows bringing in lots of sunlight, the wood counter is the perfect place to grow plants that soften what could have been an austere look.

**Pale green tiles** the color of the sea when sunlight plays on its surface bring to mind vacations in the sun. This tub is partially enclosed by the end of the shower stall and by a tall tile-covered partition that has a built-in chest of drawers on the other side. A tiled niche carved out of the wall provides a space for sponges and fragrant soaps. Frosted glass in the bottom pane of the window over the tub and at the lower part of the shower window ensure privacy.

**A large whirlpool tub** set under the peak of an upstairs bathroom has a bright blue tile surround that covers storage areas on either side of the tub. Access to the tub's working parts is through doors in the front of the surround. The light wood of the ceiling beams is repeated in the window trim and the baseboard, creating a pleasing contrast with the blue tiles. A painting over the tub ties together the blue of the tiles and the color of the wood.

**A new master bath** was created in what had been a small bedroom. Part of the wall separating the two rooms was removed and a window was cut through the remaining wall above the tub. The whirlpool tub has a classic gray and white marble surround. The colors of the marble are repeated on the walls and woodwork.

**The simple lines** of the large window in this attic bath set the stage for the clawfoot tub. The wood wainscoting extends high up the wall and is painted the same slate blue as the outside of the tub. The cream color of the upper walls sets off the white window trim, emphasizing the window's interesting shape.

**Cerulean blue tiles** line a shower enclosure that is large enough not to need a door. Two windows looking out on the owner's large property—no concerns for privacy here—bring sunlight into the shower. An interior window was installed in the shower wall to allow the light to shine on the clawfoot tub and to brighten the rest of the bathroom, painted a cheerful yellow.

**Mosaic tiles in three colors** are used to create an Art Deco design in this shower stall. The same mosaic tiles with a border of slightly larger tiles are used on the floor. The brass-trimmed shower door and glass partition allow the design to be on view from the rest of the bathroom.

**A strikingly modern** shower enclosure made of glass and marble abuts a matching marble vanity. A glass panel, the same size as the window and frosted on the lower half for privacy, was inserted in the wall at right. The shower faucet is attached to the marble above and below the window. The marble wall at the back has a shelf and a niche for toiletries. With no visible means of attachment, the glass shower door and the glass wall above the vanity look like they are floating in a sea of marble.

**The mahogany-colored** tiles and gold trim in this bathroom capture the indulgent feeling of rich materials. The shower stall is relatively small but the glass door, beige mosaic tile floor, and deep window ledge that can be used for holding soap and other necessities keep it from feeling cramped. The floor-to-ceiling mirror with its own towel bars increases the sense of space in the bathroom. Using the same rich mahogany color for the laminate vanity creates a seamless look to the room.

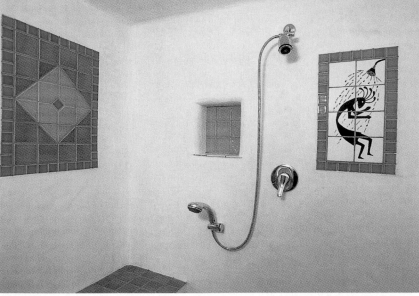

**This large adobe shower room** has both a handheld shower and a regular shower head as well as a comfortable terra-cotta-tiled bench. A wall niche, lined in turquoise tiles, can hold shampoo and other shower needs. Two tile plaques embellish the walls. One is a geometric that incorporates all three tile colors, the other a whimsical depiction of what goes on in the shower.

# Surface splendor

**Mixing but never matching** tiles are used to create this garden room complete with its own birdcage. A separate compartment for the toilet displays an urn filled with an enormous bouquet of flowers over light blue tiles set at an angle. A smaller bouquet adorns the wall to the left of the sink, which is covered with flowers that coordinate with the tile border around the vanity and the mirror. The partial wall separating the toilet and sink has a classic column swathed in a ribbon and flower garland. Anchoring all the decorative tile is a floor of octagonal terra-cotta tiles.

**This bathroom practically shouts** "rise and shine!" with its kaleidoscope of tiles in the rich colors of a desert sunset lining both the walls and the floor. The vivid geometric border and black cove tile form a separation between the tiles and the intense melon color of the walls. The tiles set off the simple lines of the pedestal sink. The small wooden table used for storage, the punched silver mirror frame, and the rag rug add lively contrasts in texture.

**The refined, neutral color** of this bathroom is created by limiting the number of materials used. The walls are covered with pale wood panels edged with molding stained slightly darker. This molding becomes sculptured towel bars on the walls at the left and right of the room. The diagonal direction of the wood-strip floor provides a sense of movement that contrasts with the serenity of the geometric wall panels. All the wood in the room creates a serene backdrop for the extra-wide pedestal sink and the freestanding bathtub. The long mirror over the sink is the same width as the wood panels and, placed vertically, sets off the horizontal bands of wood. The color and soft texture of the hooked rugs add a note of warmth.

**A textured wallpaper** that resembles a crackled paint finish is the background for the ikatlike fabric window shade and wallpaper border along the ceiling. The ceiling is painted dark brown to give the illusion of a cathedral ceiling, lending this small bathroom a more spacious feeling.

**A soft paisley fabric** in grays and beiges covers the walls of this bathroom and is used in voluminous curtains at the full-length window. Sheer curtains hang underneath the paisley ones to ensure privacy while admitting light. The walnut vanity with its marble top, the matching marble tile floor, the large ebony and gold-framed mirror, and the wall sconces add to the sophisticated decor.

**A variety of painting techniques** decorate the walls of this bathroom. A hand-painted branch with delicate leaves covers the tile tub surround and reaches to the walls above. Diamonds were painted on the walls in beige and gray using masking tape to outline the exact shapes, then white paint was applied with a rag on top of them to create a very subtle pattern. The almost diaphanous look of this pattern, complemented by the bunched sheer curtain at the window, forms a perfect background for the collection of metal picture frames.

**The marble floor inspired** the beige palette in this bathroom. The striped wallpaper picks up the soft beiges and browns of the floor, the almond fixtures, the speckled solid-surface countertop, and the blond wood vanity. The basket planter and the purple balloon window valance add texture to the room, while the valance and the curves of the vanity soften the angularity of the toilet, the square floor tiles, and the striped wallpaper.

# Abundant light

**The triple window** over the tub, simply dressed in white sheers caught up in a swag, brings beautiful sunlight into the bathroom. The light is amplified by its reflection in the large mirror over the double vanity. An under-the-eaves window introduces even more light into the room that is intensified by the many white surfaces—the fixtures, the tile floor and tub surround, the solid-surface countertop, and the long, white-stained wood vanity. Because the walls and ceiling are painted a pale cream color and the woodwork is a bright white, the bathroom seems even more spacious. A few accessories in bright colors add a warm touch and soften the shiny white surfaces.

**The majestic window** in this bright bathroom consists of a large, multipaned picture window surrounded by double-hung windows and topped with a centered, half-round fanlight. The large mirror over the vanity reflects the light streaming in. The skylight has been placed directly over the whirlpool tub so every area of this bathroom benefits from sunlight. Four tulip-shaped sconces attached to the mirror and reflected in it provide light at the vanity for tasks like shaving or applying makeup, and a chandelier in the ceiling furnishes ambient light for the entire room. White fixtures and beige textured wallpaper create a neutral backdrop for the bright blue tile countertop.

**Tucked under the eaves,** this bathroom receives a generous amount of light from the window and the skylight placed directly above it. The light is reflected in a mirror that fills one wall above the fixtures. The unusual shape of the bathroom is defined by the checkerboard band of tiles that edges the wall above the window, follows the angle of the wall up to the peak of the ceiling, and forms a border under the mirror. This crisp black-and-white tile trim adds a debonair note to this otherwise all-white room.

**With such a glorious view** of the landscape and with privacy not a concern, a picture window becomes the entire back wall of the bathroom. A skylight installed directly above the tub brings in even more light, all of which is reflected in the mirrored cabinets at the end of the tub and in the large mirror over the vanity. The colors of the decor—white cabinets and pale beige marble floor and tub surround—were kept deliberately subdued so as not to compete with the ever-changing colors of nature outside.

**Creating a separate area** for the toilet and sink provides a little more privacy in the bathroom, a nice asset but not at the expense of light. The clever use of mirrors and a glass-block wall allows light from the only window into the rest of the room. The top half of the partition is made of glass block that permits light from the window to reach the bathtub. A mirror over the sink helps reflect the light in the corner, and the large mirror on the angled wall at the right, extending from the top of the tile all the way to the ceiling, brings light into the rest of the room.

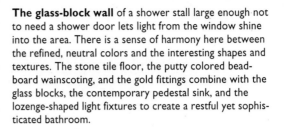

**The glass-block wall** of a shower stall large enough not to need a shower door lets light from the window shine into the area. There is a sense of harmony here between the refined, neutral colors and the interesting shapes and textures. The stone tile floor, the putty colored bead-board wainscoting, and the gold fittings combine with the glass blocks, the contemporary pedestal sink, and the lozenge-shaped light fixtures to create a restful yet sophisticated bathroom.

**One wall was bumped out** to accommodate a large whirlpool tub, and long, narrow windows were installed to fill the extra depth. The light from a large window, covered with sheer shirred curtains for privacy, is reflected in the mirror over the vanity. The same pale stone tiles are used on the floor, the tub surround, and the walls all the way up to the ceiling, creating a serene look that is complemented by the long white vanity cabinet. Recessed lights above the vanity offer task lighting for grooming, and recessed lights in the ceiling provide ambient light for the entire room.

**A universally designed** bathroom is one that is accessible to everyone regardless of their age or ability to move around. This bathroom has no barriers, not even in the large shower area. There is a seat, grab bars, and an adjustable hand-held shower head. The toilet, installed several inches higher than usual, has a grab bar along the back wall and another one that can be pulled down alongside when needed. The sink is wall mounted and the plumbing is set back, creating knee space below to accommodate a person in a wheelchair. This bathroom is well lit, has nonslip flooring, and is free of clutter—all of which help to make the room safe.

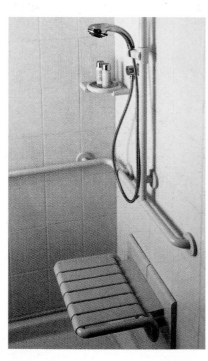

**Bathroom accessories** that are safe and user friendly include grab bars along two walls and a seat that flips up out of the way when it is not needed (left). A shiny red shower seat, grab bars, shower head, curtain rod, and soap holder (right) pack a powerful design punch in this bathroom.

**Often, making a single change** in a bathroom can create a room that is much more accessible and easier to use. In this bathroom, a new shower was installed that is large enough to include a fold-down seat and a grab bar. It is finished with easy-to-maintain ceramic tile that coordinates with the tile used throughout the room. The bathroom floor is covered with a textured ceramic tile to prevent falls and there is ample space to move around between the sink and the other fixtures. The room is well lit, with sunlight coming in through the window over the bathtub and recessed downlights providing illumination at the sink, shower, and bathtub.

# A guest's retreat

**A powder room** can often be decorated more sumptuously than a full bathroom because heat and moisture are not an issue. This one has been given the Midas touch with gold-foil wallpaper covering the walls and ceiling. The black sink, seen reflected in the large mirror over the mirrored vanity shelf, provides a striking contrast to the gold. Most of the accessories, including the perfume bottles on the vanity, the framed painting over the sink, the small seat next to it, and the wall sconces, carry through the gold theme.

**A garden of delights** has been created in this half bath with its trompe l'oeil painting of a stone wall and trellis filled with a vine of ivy leaves. The vine climbs across the top of the vanity and creeps down its front. The trellis surrounds the beautiful octagonal leaded-glass window. Beyond the painted wall is a hint of a field of wildflowers waiting to be explored. The pale green sink and toilet, topped with a real vine, and the vanity the color of stone add to the illusion that this is indeed a garden to enjoy in private .

**An antique gold mirror** and wall sconces over a classically styled pedestal sink form the focus of this half bath and are complemented by the pale gold striped wallpaper and marble tile wall.

**Only the essential elements** are here, highlighted by a beautifully crafted wood storage closet, rich marble floor tiles, and an elegant, silver-trimmed mirror and wall sconces. To fit the fixtures into this tiny space, the toilet was placed at an angle and a small pedestal sink was installed.

**A gazebo welcomes visitors** in this guest bathroom. The trompe l'oeil curtains and awning-striped tent top reveal an imaginative garden beyond, which can be seen reflected in the gold-framed mirror. The lovely oval window, which is also visible in the mirror, was the inspiration for this whimsical design. The decorative boxes and mirror frames, all painted in gold and trimmed in black, are in keeping with the personality of the room.

**A cabinet with a sink**
on top is standard bath-
room storage, but here
the classic pilasters and
raised-panel doors give
the cabinet a more ele-
gant look. This white
enamel-painted cabinet
has discreet brass knobs
that repeat the other
brass items like the wall
sconces, the mirror
frame, and the fittings.
The white solid-surface
countertop, with its un-
dermounted sink, is large
enough for more storage
or for displaying favorite
toiletries. The separate
compartment for the
toilet is outfitted with a
built-in bookcase to hold
reading material.

**Mirrored drawers and cabinet doors** on the vanity reflect the beautiful floral rug on the floor, and antique crystal doorpulls coordinate with the crystal light fixture. The vanity provides ample storage space and is large enough for two sculptured sinks with plenty of counter space between them.

**The black solid-surface countertop** around this sink tops a vanity containing drawers and a cabinet. The same material forms the graceful, curving bathtub surround and continues to the back wall, where it becomes a shelf for plants or a window seat. More storage cabinets are tucked under the seat below the window and under the seat next to the sink.

**Adding a wall to create** a private compartment for the toilet produced a niche for the vanity that gives it a built-in look. The white-tiled countertop holds a decorative sink that is large enough for the three storage sections below it. The mirror covers the entire length of the back wall so the vanity can be shared by two people.

**Utilizing any space for storage,** no matter how small, makes a bathroom more useful. In this small bathroom, towel bars were installed between wall studs, creating much-needed storage next to the vanity.

**The rough wood** of this custom-built vanity that holds two sinks is finished with a brick-colored stain. Its majestic size and interesting shape with turned pilasters at the ends belie its utilitarian purpose— to provide storage and to hide the plumbing. The storage here consists of two closed shelves and an open cubby for towels.

**Cabinets of varying sizes** and shapes are put together to form a storage unit. A tall cabinet on the right for towels and a cabinet on the left for the sink are bridged by a lower shelf used as a dressing table, with drawers for storing beauty products. Vertical incandescent lights on the sides of the mirror provide good lighting. A high shelf has closed storage as well as open areas for display. A small antique dresser near the tub has been painted to coordinate with the wall unit.

**Bold and modern** above-the-counter sinks demand equally bold storage units. The small three-drawer cabinets here are used for storing toiletries, and the large cabinet in the center is for towels and cleaning supplies. The tables that support the sinks, the frames of the mirrors above the wall-hung faucets, and all three cabinets are finished with a dark stain that contrasts with the bright white china sinks and countertops.

**A freestanding pine cabinet** between two pedestal sinks has a countertop made of the same green tiles used on the walls. Above the cabinet are glass shelves set into a recess in the wall. The tile countertop and the placement of the cabinet in front of the recess combine to give it a built-in look. The cabinet and shelves provide plenty of storage space for supplies for the two sinks.

# PLANNING GUIDELINES

The bathroom is probably the most frequently used room in the house but one that's often taken for granted. Careful planning can help you create a design that will turn your bathroom into a perfect retreat. Here's how to get started.

First, you want to take a good look at your present bathroom and take inventory of the room. Determine what works and what doesn't and which elements you want to keep. Then decide on the extent of the remodel. Will you freshen the room with paint and wallpaper, replace old fixtures, move walls to enlarge the bathroom, or add much-needed storage?

Next, dream about what you want and educate yourself in the process. Start a file of photographs and information from advertisements, manufacturers' product literature, shelter magazines, trade publications, newspapers. Use the Internet to visit Web sites of manufacturers, shelter magazines, trade groups. Visit stores and showrooms, model homes, recently remodeled bathrooms of friends, and home improvement stores to see what is available. Keep a notebook, organized by subject, such as layouts and plans, color, fixtures, faucets, flooring, and so on. Based on the information that you have gathered, list everything you would like to have.

Lastly, sketch your ideas on a floor plan. Choose fixtures, a vanity, and flooring. Create a sample board. Put samples of paint, tile, flooring, and fixture finishes on a posterboard and live with it for a while to see how you like your choices.

This chapter reviews the entire remodeling process—from initial planning to final design—so select and adapt the ideas here that apply to your own project, and enjoy.

# Getting started

## A BATHROOM INVENTORY

The first step in any bathroom remodel is to analyze your present bathroom. The success of the new room depends on how well it suits your family's needs—the way it works for the people who use it. It's important to know not only what you want but also what you don't want, to identify things you'd like to improve, to evaluate the room's strengths and weaknesses, and then to set goals for remodeling. By answering the questions below, you will have a clearer idea of what you would like and be able to assign priorities to those improvements.

**Layout**. Consider your bathroom's layout to decide if a different configuration of toilet, sink, and bathtub would be more suitable.

- ❏ *Is your bathroom in a convenient location?*
- ❏ *Does the door open into the room? If so, will it inconvenience someone inside? When open, do cabinet or vanity doors and drawers block the door?*
- ❏ *Can two people use the sink or vanity area at the same time? Is the vanity mirror large enough?*
- ❏ *Would your family benefit from the added privacy of a compartmentalized bathroom, with tub, shower, or toilet separate from each other and from the vanity?*
- ❏ *Is there ample room for toweling dry without hitting elbows?*
- ❏ *Are stored items within easy reach?*

**Fixtures and fittings.** Before you decide to buy new fixtures and fittings, consider whether the existing ones can be cleaned, refinished, or repaired.

- ❏ *What features do you like and dislike about your current equipment?*
- ❏ *Are you pleased with the sizes, shapes, and materials?*
- ❏ *Are the faucets easy to turn on and off with soapy hands?*
- ❏ *Is there room to wash your hair in the sink? To hand wash delicate clothing?*
- ❏ *Can you adjust water temperature for the sink and shower as easily as you'd like? Would you like a fixture that regulates the water temperature?*
- ❏ *Do family members like to take a bath, a shower, or both?*
- ❏ *Would you like to add a whirlpool bath?*

**Walls, floor, and ceiling.** Moisture is the enemy of most room surfaces and subsurfaces. Water causes floors to warp, paint to deteriorate, and wallpaper to peel. Choose new surface materials not only for color and texture but also for moisture resistance, easy maintenance, and durability.

- ❏ *Do the surfaces in your present bathroom have chips, cracks, bubbles, mold, or mildew? Are there any leaks?*
- ❏ *Is paint or wallpaper peeling?*
- ❏ *Is the tile uneven? Are the grout and caulking in good condition? Have any subsurfaces been damaged by excess moisture?*

**Countertops.** More counter space is one of the primary requests of a bathroom renovation, one that will make the room more pleasant and more efficient.

- ❏ *Do you have ample and conveniently located counter space in your bathroom?*
- ❏ *Do you need more room for storage or display? Is your bathroom simply lacking a convenient place to put things down?*
- ❏ *Are existing countertops in good condition? Are joints and corners easy to keep clean? Would you prefer a different countertop material?*

**Storage.** Before you plan new storage, it's a good idea to clean out and organize your bathroom's existing storage areas to determine what you need.

- ❏ *Are items you use daily conveniently located? Is the storage easy to use as well as accessible?*
- ❏ *Is there a place to store medicines and cleaning supplies away from children?*
- ❏ *Would you like a recessed medicine cabinet, better storage for cleaning supplies, a place for dirty laundry, or a convenient spot for your bathroom scale?*
- ❏ *Would you like to add a vanity, wall cabinets, or a floor-to-ceiling unit complete with shelves and bins?*
- ❏ *Will the layout of your home allow you to enlarge the room to gain space?*
- ❏ *Is it possible to store some items in a hall closet or other nearby space?*

**Lighting.** Older bathrooms rarely have enough properly placed light fixtures—often only one overhead light or a single fixture above the medicine cabinet.

- ❏ *Do you need to upgrade general lighting?*
- ❏ *Would you like to add task lighting for shaving or putting on makeup?*
- ❏ *Are you pleased with the appearance of existing light fixtures, and is the kind of light (fluorescent or incandescent) what you want?*
- ❏ *Can you bring in more natural light? Can you add a skylight, enlarge an existing window, or create a new window?*

**Electrical outlets and switches.** Note the location and number of electrical outlets and switches in your bathroom. Plan to substitute ground-fault circuit interrupter (GFCI) outlets for standard plugs in all wet areas in the bathroom.

- ❑ *Are there enough outlets? Are switches and outlets conveniently placed? Are they located safely away from wet areas?*
- ❑ *Do you want to replace a single outlet with a double one?*
- ❑ *In a large space, would two- or three-way switches for lights be more convenient?*

**Heating and ventilation.** Controlled temperature and good ventilation are basic for bathroom comfort.

- ❑ *Is your bathroom too chilly in the morning? Do you want to add a radiant lamp or heated towel bars?*
- ❑ *Do you have to stop to wipe off a foggy mirror while shaving? Do you gasp for air in the middle of a steamy shower? Do you have an exhaust fan?*
- ❑ *Is the ventilation sufficient so the air is healthy to breathe and the moisture dissipates quickly?*
- ❑ *Do you have a problem with mold or mildew?*

### A home spa

Adding a luxurious amenity like a steam shower or sauna lets you create a spa in your own home.

A steam shower uses a generator that's small enough to be housed in a vanity or storage cabinet to generate hot, moist air in the space of a conventional shower. It's possible to retrofit an existing shower; you will need a generator, control pad, airtight shower door, comfortable bench, waterproof and steam-resistant surround, and effective ventilation.

The sauna, which originated in Finland, is a small wood-lined room (usually sold prefabricated) equipped with a heater topped with lava rocks that creates hot, dry heat. The walls, ceiling, floor, and built-in benches are made of a soft wood such as redwood or cedar. In addition to the room and heater, you will need a thermostat, timer, lights, and inlet and outlet vents.

**Water and energy conservation.** Heating the bathroom and the water used in the bathroom consume a lot of energy.

- ❑ *Are the water heater, pipes, and walls well insulated?*
- ❑ *Is the shower head equipped with a flow restrictor or shut-off valve?*
- ❑ *If you have an older toilet still in good condition, do you want to consider replacing it with a new, low-flush model?*

**Privacy.** Privacy in the bathroom is of paramount importance, so consider ways to increase it, if you need to.

- ❑ *Does the door of your bathroom open to a public area? If so, can you relocate the opening?*
- ❑ *Does a window open to a public area? If so, can you replace it with a window of frosted glass or design an exterior treatment to increase privacy?*
- ❑ *Can you hear sounds of running water? Do you have uninsulated or plastic pipes, finishing materials that reflect sound, or insufficient floor, wall, or ceiling insulation?*

**Accessories.** Make a list of your bathroom accessories and note any additions or changes you'd like to make in their quality, quantity, or style.

- ❑ *Do you have sufficient towel bars, and are they conveniently placed?*
- ❑ *Do you want the finish on towel bars, mirror frames, and cabinet hardware to match existing or new fittings?*
- ❑ *Would accessories in a new material such as glass, ceramic, or brightly colored plastic brighten the room?*
- ❑ *Do your doors and drawers need new hardware? Are the handles comfortable to use?*

**Maintenance.** Some bathrooms are easier to maintain than others. By choosing materials especially designed to withstand moisture, you can make the room easier to clean.

- ❑ *Can you install smooth, seamless or jointless materials (except flooring)?*
- ❑ *Does your layout eliminate nooks and difficult-to-reach spots?*
- ❑ *Are your fixtures difficult to clean?*
- ❑ *Do any fixtures need to be refinished or replaced?*

**Family needs.** A bathroom should be convenient for everyone to use. Take time to consider the special needs of family members and regular visitors, including children and elderly or disabled persons.

- ❑ *Can an adult bathe a small child safely and comfortably?*
- ❑ *Is the tub or shower equipped with a nonskid base and grab bars?*
- ❑ *If wheelchair access is a consideration, is the entry wide enough, and is there ample space for easy turning?*
- ❑ *Can all the fixtures be used without assistance? (For more information on universal design and barrier-free fixtures, see pages 26–27 and 50.)*

# Developing your plan

Before you begin a bathroom remodel, you'll need to measure the room and draw it to scale. The process of measuring the bathroom elements and perimeter will increase your awareness of the existing space. Scale drawings also serve as a foundation for future design and may satisfy the permit requirements of your local building department. Such plans will also help you communicate your ideas to any professional you hire. And you'll save money by providing a professional with these measurements and drawings.

There are a few ways to create a floor plan. You can purchase one of the design kits that come with graph paper and scale drawings of bathroom fixtures to create a layout. If you're computer savvy, a number of companies produce design software that enables you to create floor plans and elevations, or straight-on views of each wall, easily and quickly with measurements from your bathroom. And computer-aided design (CAD) software lets you see how a room looks in three dimensions and allows you to move walls and windows and drag fixtures in and out.

On these pages you'll learn how you can measure your bathroom, record those measurements, and draw a two-dimensional floor plan to scale.

## Tools for measuring

You can find these items at hardware, stationery, or art supply stores.

- Retractable steel measuring tape or folding wooden rule
- Ruler or T-square
- Triangle
- Compass
- Graph paper (four squares to an inch)
- Masking tape

## MEASURING YOUR BATHROOM

Before you begin taking measurements, draw a rough sketch of the bathroom, its various elements, and any adjacent areas that may be included in the remodeling. Make the sketch as large as the paper allows so you'll have room to write in dimensions. Note any deviations from the standard wall and partition thickness (usually about 5 inches). And make sure the sketch shows all aspects of the room, including projections, recesses, windows, doors, and door swings.

**How to measure.** It's important to record the dimensions on the sketch as you measure, using feet and inches as an architect would (you may also want

## BEFORE

The original floor plan shows a typical bathroom with basic fixtures and very little room for grooming. Natural light is provided by one window opposite the door and artificial light by two fixtures, one in the ceiling and one next to the sink. Storage is limited to space under the sink.

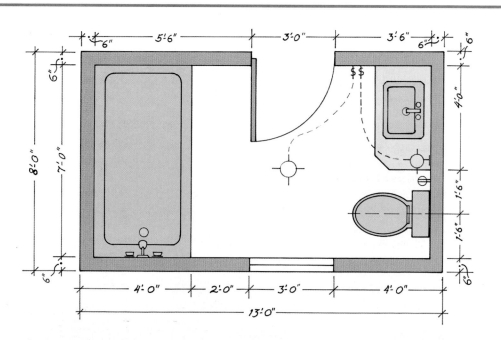

to translate certain dimensions, such as those for tubs and shower enclosures, to inches). Measure to the nearest ⅛ inch, since even a fraction of an inch counts in fitting and spacing bathroom elements. All measurements should be taken up to the wall, not to any projecting wood trim or baseboards.

First, measure the bathroom's dimensions—the floor, ceiling, and walls; measure each wall at counter height. Note down the measurements.

To find out if the bathroom is square, measure the diagonals (corner to opposite corner). Don't worry if the room isn't square; just be sure your drawing reflects any irregularities.

Next, with the overall dimensions on your sketch, measure the fixtures and other elements in the room and the distances between them, and add this information to your sketch. You can use a wall-by-wall approach or you can measure by category: fixtures, doors, windows, cabinetry, shelves, and accessories.

Finally, depending on the extent of your remodel, include in your sketch locations of the following: load-bearing walls and partitions, electrical outlets and switches, light fixtures, drains, pipes, and vents. If you want to enlarge your bathroom—or just add more storage space—show adjacent hall space, closets, rooms, and outdoor areas that you may be able to incorporate into your new floor plan.

Note heights such as the clearance space under a duct or sloping ceiling, the soffit space, the floor-to-ceiling height, and the distance from the floor to the tops and bottoms of the windows.

## DRAWING FLOOR PLANS TO SCALE

To create a useful floor plan and elevations you need a well-prepared sketch with accurate measurements and the

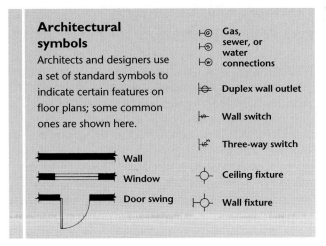

### Architectural symbols

Architects and designers use a set of standard symbols to indicate certain features on floor plans; some common ones are shown here.

- Wall
- Window
- Door swing
- Gas, sewer, or water connections
- Duplex wall outlet
- Wall switch
- Three-way switch
- Ceiling fixture
- Wall fixture

ability to convert those measurements to the scale you choose. Your drawings don't have to be beautiful, but they should be prepared carefully so they are precise, complete, and easy to read.

Though architects sometimes use a ¼-inch scale—that is, ¼ inch on the drawings equals 1 foot in the actual room—using a ½-inch scale for your bathroom drawings is easier, especially when you want to include all the elements of the room and have room to write their dimensions.

**How to draw floor plans.** With masking tape, attach the corners of the graph paper to a smooth working surface.

Use a straightedge such as a ruler, T-square, or triangle to draw all horizontal and vertical lines; make right angles exact. Use a compass to indicate door swings.

To complete the floor plan, refer to your sketch and the sample finished floor plan shown below. Indicate walls and partitions with dark, thick lines to make the floor plan easier to read.

## AFTER

The new floor plan shows how additional space was created by moving the outside wall about 3 feet to accommodate a new shower and toilet alcove. A pocket door closes off this space, providing privacy so another person can use the sink or tub. New fixtures include a 5- by 5-foot platform tub and two deck-mounted sinks in an extended countertop with ample storage underneath. This plan includes new lighting fixtures for each area and new electrical outlets.

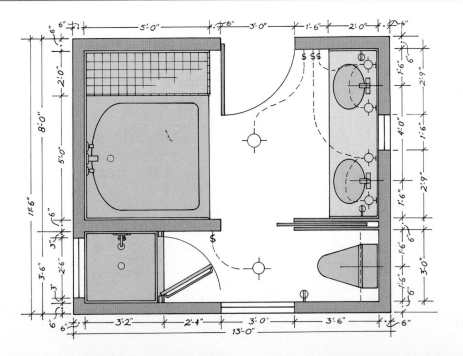

# Basic layouts

There is no one perfect design for a bathroom—layouts vary dramatically according to taste, style, and size. A good, workable floor plan, however, will provide for good access into the room, easy movement within the room, fixtures that are convenient to use, and plenty of accessible storage.

Once you've reviewed your present bathroom's good points and drawbacks, it's time to start planning your new one. While brainstorming ideas for your bathroom, try to have some basic layout schemes in mind. The floor plans shown below, arranged by type of bathroom, provide a starting point. Keep in mind that these layouts can be combined, adapted, and expanded to meet your needs.

## POWDER ROOM

Whether you call it a guest bath, half bath, or a powder room, this room contains a toilet and a sink and perhaps some limited storage space. Because it's used only occasionally and for short intervals, you can be more creative when decorating a powder room, using less durable and possibly more extravagant finishes. The door should open against a wall, clear of any fixtures. Where space is tight, consider a very small sink or a pocket door, and create the illusion of space with mirrors and lighting.

Privacy is important. A guest bath should open off a hallway, not directly into the living room, family room, or dining area.

## FAMILY BATH

Three fixtures—a toilet, a sink, and a bathtub or shower or combination tub/shower—are the mainstay of a family bath. The fixture arrangement can vary depending on the size and shape of the room, which should be a minimum of 5 feet by 7 feet.

To enable several family members to use the bathroom at the same time, consider putting in two sinks or compartmentalizing separate fixture areas. One way is to isolate the toilet and shower from the sink and grooming area, which increases privacy when it's not feasible to add a new bathroom.

The family bath is one of the most frequently used rooms in the house, so choose durable, moisture-resistant, easy-to-clean fixtures and finishes, and plan adequate storage space for each user's needs.

## CHILDREN'S BATH

Think safety first and easy maintenance second when designing a bathroom for children. Use slip-resistant

## SAMPLE BATHROOM LAYOUTS

**POWDER ROOM**
4' by 4'-6"

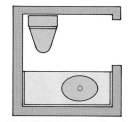

**POWDER ROOM** 5' by 5'

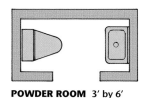

**POWDER ROOM** 3' by 6'

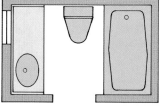

**FAMILY BATH** 5' by 7'

**FAMILY BATH** 7' by 11'

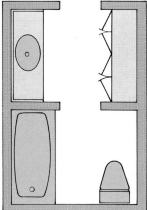

**FAMILY BATH** 8' by 12'

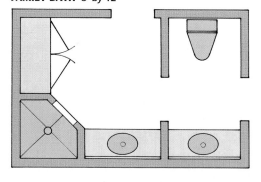

**BACK-TO-BACK** 5' by 7' each

surfaces to prevent accidents, pressure-balanced faucets to reduce the chances of a hot-water burn, and a timer on the light switch to keep electrical bills down. Plastic laminate countertops and cabinets are a good choice— they're durable and easy to clean. For more information on safety, see page 45.

In a bath for two, if there's space you may want to consider shared bath and toilet facilities and an individual sink for each child. When several children are sharing one bath, having color coded drawers, towel hooks, and other storage areas can help minimize territorial battles. Some bathrooms are located between two children's bedrooms, with direct access from each room.

## MASTER BATH SUITE

No longer a utilitarian space, today's master bath can be a serene retreat reflecting the personality and interests of its owners. Often it includes individual dressing and grooming areas with dual sinks, a distinct area for the toilet, and separate tub and shower facilities. Amenities include fireplaces, whirlpool baths, oversize tubs, and bidets. Access to the outside can provide a sunbathing deck or private garden.

For your master bath, you may want to consider a walk-in dressing room, an exercise room, a makeup center, a reading nook, a greenhouse, and even a home entertainment center. You may also want to think about

a sauna or a steam shower (see page 37). If you do, make sure you provide adequate ventilation to prevent water damage to any equipment and accessories.

## UNIVERSAL BATH

When remodeling, consider the needs of everyone who will use the bath—children, a disabled or elderly person, as well as your own future needs. A universal or barrier-free bath requires certain heights, clearances, and room dimensions, and a room that accommodates a wheelchair has its own specific clearances (see page 50 for details). A universal bathroom will increase the resale value of your house when you decide to sell it.

For more information about universal design, contact:

Adaptive Environments Center, Inc.
374 Congress St., Suite 301
Boston, MA 02210
(617) 695-1225
www.adaptenv.org

The Center for Universal Design
School of Design
North Carolina State University, Box 8613
Raleigh, NC 27695-8613
(800) 647-6777
www.ncsu.edu/ncsu/design/cud

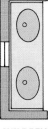
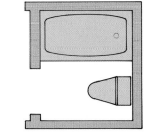

**CHILDREN'S BATH** 6' by 10'

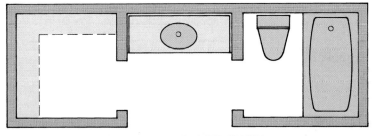

**COMPARTMENTALIZED CORRIDOR BATH WITH CLOSET**
16' by 5'

**CHILDREN'S BATH** 8' by 12'

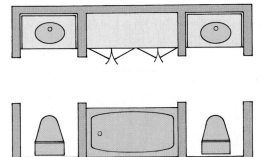

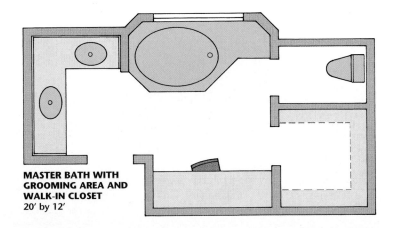

**MASTER BATH WITH GROOMING AREA AND WALK-IN CLOSET**
20' by 12'

It's important to understand some basic facts about plumbing lines, minimum heights and clearances, and fixture location before you can actually plan your bathroom layout and place your fixtures. Only then can you plan a layout that makes sense both structurally and economically. Once you have all the facts at hand, you'll be ready to experiment with layouts.

## THE EXISTING STRUCTURE

You will simplify construction and keep costs down if you select a layout that uses the existing water supply, drain lines, and vent stack. If that's not possible, you may want to study the Remodeling Basics section beginning on page 64 to familiarize yourself with the work that plumbing, wiring, and structural changes entail.

If you're adding on to your house, try to locate the new bathroom near an existing one or near the kitchen to take advantage of existing plumbing lines. It's also more economical to arrange fixtures against one or two walls, eliminating the need for additional plumbing lines.

In most cases, you can move a sink a few inches from its present position with only minor plumbing changes. Your existing supply and drain lines can usually support a second sink. You can extend existing supply and drain lines if the distance from the vent is less than the maximum distance allowed by your local code; if not, you'll have to install a secondary vent, which is a major undertaking.

If your bathroom has a wood floor with a crawlspace, basement, or first floor underneath, it's relatively simple to move both plumbing and wiring. But in rooms with concrete floors, it's an expensive proposition to move plumbing or wiring that's located under the concrete. To gain access to the lines, you would have to go through the laborious process of breaking up and removing the concrete.

Structural changes, especially those entailing work on load-bearing walls, fall into the category of serious remodeling and may require professional help. Relocating a door or window opening may also involve a lot of work, including framing and finishing. Adding a partition wall, on the other hand, is an easier and less expensive job.

## MINIMUM CLEARANCES

**Building and plumbing** codes specify minimum clearances between bathroom fixtures. Local codes may vary somewhat, but the clearances shown here are typical. Always check your local building and plumbing codes before you begin to work on a layout for your new bathroom.

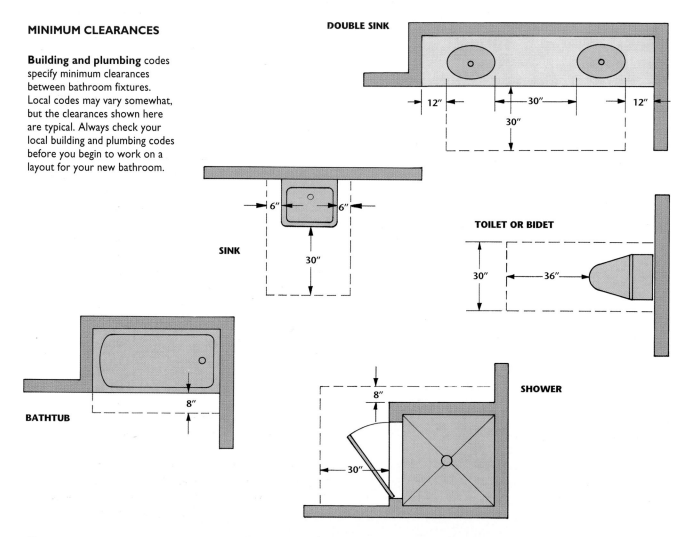

## STANDARD HEIGHTS

**These standard heights** for countertops, shower heads, and accessories can be customized to your own needs and those of others using the bathroom if you are especially tall or short. When planning such a change, however, keep in mind your home's resale value; potential buyers may not find these alterations to their liking.

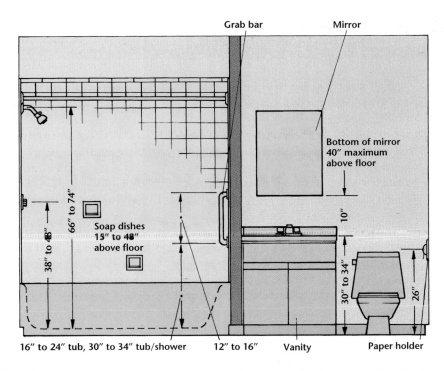

Grab bar     Mirror

Bottom of mirror 40" maximum above floor

66" to 74"

38" to 48"

Soap dishes 15" to 48" above floor

10"

30" to 34"

26"

16" to 24" tub, 30" to 34" tub/shower    12" to 16"    Vanity    Paper holder

## HEIGHTS AND CLEARANCES

Building codes specify minimum required clearances between, beside, and in front of bathroom fixtures to allow adequate room for use, cleaning, and repair. To help in your initial planning, check your local building code for the minimum clearances in your area. Examples of such clearances are shown on the facing page.

Generally, you can locate side-by-side fixtures closer together than fixtures positioned opposite each other. If a sink is opposite a bathtub or toilet, allow a minimum of 30 inches between them. Children, elderly, and disabled persons may require assistance or special fixtures. For specifications on universal design or barrier-free bathrooms, see page 50.

There are also standard heights for countertops, shower heads, and accessories. If you and others using the bathroom are especially tall or short, you may wish to customize the room to your own requirements. However, when planning such a change, you want to think about your home's resale value; potential buyers may not find these alterations as convenient as you do.

## FIXTURE ARRANGEMENT

When you begin to position the fixtures, start first with the largest unit—the bathtub or shower. Be sure you allow space for convenient access, for cleaning, and, if needed, for bathing a child.

Next, place the sink (or sinks). Since this is the most frequently used fixture in the bathroom, it should be positioned out of the traffic pattern. Be sure to plan for ample room in front for reaching below the sink, and allow plenty of elbow room at the sides.

Try to locate the toilet (and bidet, if you have one) away from the door. Typically, the toilet is placed beside the tub or shower, and a toilet and bidet are placed next to each other.

Remember to consider the swing radius for doors and windows (if they open into the bathroom). If the swing of the door conflicts with your placement of fixtures, you can either reverse a standard door's hardware from left to right or substitute a pocket door.

## EXPERIMENTING WITH LAYOUTS

To begin creating layouts, trace the scale floor plan of your existing bathroom and include any adjoining space you're planning to incorporate into the new bathroom. If you're considering removing or relocating walls, eliminate those existing partitions.

Keep track of your ideas so you can compare the various options later. One way to do this is to move paper cutouts around on the floor plan and then sketch the best plans you devise with them. To use this method, first draw the perimeter of your existing floor plan and any adjacent areas to be included in the project. Then, using graph paper, make cutouts to scale of fixtures, cabinets, countertops, and other elements—both existing features you plan to keep and new ones to be added. Move the cutouts around on the floor plan; when you hit on a layout you like, sketch it so you'll have a record of it. When you're ready, you can compare the various plans and evaluate the advantages and disadvantages of each before you settle on a new layout.

You can also make layouts using a design kit that includes graph paper and ready-made cutouts to scale. You can arrange and rearrange the cutouts, and when you are pleased with an arrangement, sketch the layout.

If you're comfortable with the computer, another way to create layouts is to use a software program specifically designed for creating floor plans. When you have a design that you like, you just print it out. When you have several designs you like, you can compare and contrast them.

With a basic layout chosen, it's time to fine-tune your plan. Begin by drawing an elevation of each bathroom wall, a straight-on view of each wall showing the visual pattern created by all the elements against that wall. Mark on those elevations the fixtures you've already located. Then you can add other elements that go into the bathroom: storage, mirrors, towel bars, amenities, and heating and ventilation details.

To do this, you can use cutouts of straight-on views of cabinets, mirrors, and other elements. Arrange these cutouts on the elevation with an eye for the overall design. The plans you sketch as you move the cutouts around will help you visualize the room as a whole. Be sure to set aside the sketches you like so you can compare them later. Or, if you prefer to work on your computer, you can use a design software program.

## STORAGE NEEDS

Think about what you need to store, how much space you need for it, and how best to organize the space. Consider equipping a vanity or cabinet with racks, shelves, pullouts, or lazy Susans for supplies. Many bathroom items such as colorful towels or stacks of soap can be displayed on open storage. If space is tight, plan to add recessed shelving between the studs. For a look at a variety of successful storage solutions, see pages 30–33.

## FILLING IN THE DETAILS

Your choice of fixtures, fittings, and cabinetry will create the overall look of your bathroom, but finishing touches can make it more appealing and comfortable. Consider the following areas.

**Surfaces.** Floor, wall, and countertop surfaces should be durable as well as attractive. For details about various surface materials, see pages 55 and 62–63.

**Lighting.** Plan your lighting as part of the initial design. A wide range of incandescent, fluorescent, and halogen light sources and fixtures to house them are available. For more information, see pages 48–49.

**Electrical outlets and switches.** Tentatively mark the locations of outlets and switches. Every countertop longer than 12 inches should have a two-plug outlet; every wall must have an outlet every 12 feet. Keep light switches at least 5 feet from the tub or shower. Be sure all outlets in the bathroom are grounded and protected with GFCI circuit breakers. Place switches 44 inches above the floor on the open (or latch) side of doorways.

**Hardware and accessories.** For an integrated overall look, think about how you'll coordinate doorknobs, drawer pulls, towel bars, a toilet-paper holder, and other accessories with your fixtures, fittings, and surfaces.

## HEATING AND VENTILATION

If you want to extend your existing heating system to a new bathroom, check with a professional to be sure your system can handle the added load. You can relocate a hot-air register in the floor or in the vanity kickspace by changing the ductwork beneath the floor; ducts for wall registers can be rerouted in a stud wall. If you're adding a register, locate it where the ductwork can be extended easily from the existing system and where you won't sacrifice wall space.

Hot-air ductwork is best done by a heating or sheet-metal contractor. Extending hot water or steam systems is easier, but it too calls for professional help. It may be more practical to equip your bathroom with an electric space heater, which can be recessed in the wall or ceiling, or with an electric heat lamp. If you are putting in a new ceramic tile floor, this is a good time to add radiant floor heating

Local building codes may require exhaust fans in certain bathrooms and specify their placement; check the code before you complete your design. Such fans are relatively simple to add or relocate. The units are installed in the ceiling between joists or in the wall between studs, and may require ductwork to the outside.

### ELEVATION DRAWING

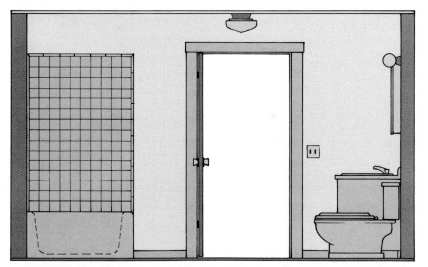

**An elevation drawing** is actually a preview of the new arrangement of structural elements, fixtures, and storage units. Because this preview is on paper, you can rearrange it to try new ideas before you begin any work.

# Playing it safe in the bathroom

More home accidents occur in the bathroom than in any other single room in the house. Although children and the elderly are the most vulnerable, you don't have to be old or young to be at risk. Bathrooms present opportunities for accidents with wet tile floors, bare feet, hot water, and electric grooming tools. You can reduce the risk of injury by careful planning and by encouraging safe practices. Listed below are some guidelines.

❑ Install sufficient lighting. Include a night-light, especially if you have young children.

❑ Choose tempered glass, plastic, and other shatterproof materials for construction and accessories.

❑ Install locks that can be opened from the outside in an emergency.

❑ Locate shelves and hooks above eye level. Install self-closing cabinet hinges and drawers to avoid having doors left open.

❑ Select a tub or shower with a nonslip surface. For existing fixtures, use a rubber bath mat.

❑ Install L-shaped or horizontal grab bars, capable of supporting a person weighing 300 pounds, in tub, shower, and toilet areas. Installation must be done properly—bracing with lumber between studs may be required. Only accessories mounted into the studs provide sufficient support.

❑ Choose slip-resistant flooring with a textured or matte finish. Anchor any carpeting. Choose area rugs or bath mats with nonskid backing.

❑ If you are installing a stall shower, make it 42 inches in at least one direction, even if local codes allow for a 36-inch square, to have

**Safety devices** in the bathroom make it easier for the young, the old, and anyone in between to use the fixtures safely and help prevent injuries. Accessories for the bathtub include a seat, safety bars, and a temperature-limiting mixing valve at the faucet. Tools for the shower include a seat that can be raised flat against the wall when not in use, grab bars, and an adjustable shower head. The devices come in an array of colors that coordinate with any bathroom design.

sufficient space to wash without bumping into the walls or door.

❑ Avoid scalding by lowering the setting of your water heater. Or install a temperature-limiting mixing valve, which keeps the water at the temperature you've selected, or a pressure-balancing valve, which automatically adjusts the balance of hot and cold water if water is turned on elsewhere, to prevent sudden temperature drops.

❑ Test the water temperature before stepping into a shower or tub and when assisting a child or elderly person. Place shower controls where they can be accessed quickly and conveniently.

❑ Be sure electrical outlets are grounded and protected with GFCI circuit breakers. Outlets should be out of reach from the shower or

bathtub. Install safety covers over unused outlets.

❑ Avoid using electrical appliances in wet areas. Keep portable heaters out of the bathroom.

❑ If children live in or visit your house, buy medicines (and, when possible, household cleansers) in childproof containers. Store these items and razors in a cabinet equipped with a safety latch or lock. Tape seldom-used nonsafety containers closed. (Check the contents of your medicine cabinet at least twice a year and discard any outdated medicines. Replace any medicine that has unreadable or incomplete directions.)

❑ Keep a first-aid kit handy for use in an emergency. Post phone numbers of the nearest emergency rescue unit and poison control center.

# Design ideas

Designing a bathroom has its own special considerations because the room is hard working, takes abuse from heat and water, and usually has to serve the needs of more than one person. As with other rooms in your house, the design of your bathroom is a reflection of your style and personality, but it also has to function well.

You can design a bathroom around a particular style or period such as Early American or Art Deco, taking cues from other rooms in your house. You could create a theme based on a favorite motif, or let materials you like, such as stone, tile, or stainless steel, set the tone.

What makes a bathroom design successful? A bathroom that is attractive to look at, one that functions as it is supposed to and, most of all, one that is pleasing to you are the keys to a successful design.

## LINE, SHAPE, AND SCALE

Line, shape, and the proportion and arrangement of these elements affect the visual space of a bathroom.

**Line.** Most bathrooms incorporate many different kinds of lines, but one usually characterizes the design. Vertical lines give a sense of height, horizontals add width, diagonals suggest movement, and curved and angular lines impart a sense of grace and dynamism.

Repeating similar lines gives the room a sense of unity. Look at one of your elevation sketches. How do the vertical lines created by the vanity, windows, doors, mirrors, and shower or tub fit together? Do the horizontal lines of the window align with the tops of the shower stall, door, and mirror? Not everything can or should line up perfectly, but the effect is far more pleasing if a number of elements are aligned, particularly when they're the highest features in the room.

**Shape.** Continuity and compatibility in shape also contribute to a unified design, within reason. The same shape repeated throughout the room can become monotonous. Study the shapes created by doorways, windows, fixtures, and other elements, as well as the patterns in your flooring, wall covering, shower curtain, and towels. Consider ways to complement existing shapes or add compatible new ones. For example, if there's an arch over a recessed bathtub, create an arch over a doorway or repeat the arch on the trim of a shelf.

**Scale.** When the scale of bathroom elements is in proportion to the overall size of the room, the design feels harmonious. A small bath seems even smaller if equipped with large fixtures and a big vanity. But the same bathroom appears larger, or at least in scale, when equipped with space-saving fixtures, a small vanity, and open shelves.

Consider the proportions of adjacent features as well. When wall cabinets or linen shelves extend to the ceiling,

they often make a room seem top-heavy—and therefore smaller. To minimize this effect, you can balance the height with more weight—in color or texture—on the bottom part of the room. Look at your floor plan and elevation drawings to see if they suggest to you other ways you can modify the scale of different elements to improve the design.

## CHOOSING YOUR COLORS

Color is an exciting, versatile, and easy-to-use design tool. The size and orientation of your bathroom, your personal preferences, and the mood you want to create all affect color selection. Here are some color guidelines to help you make choices.

**A contemporary design** includes a rectangular sink with an overhanging bowl set in a sleek white cabinet that includes a great deal of storage. Reflected in the large mirror above the sink is the shower enclosure composed of glass blocks. The white fixtures, black countertop, and glass-block wall add to the modern look.

**A classic look** for this bathroom starts with a wall-hung sink that has a very high backsplash. The brass faucet, undersink supports, and other accessories add even more warmth to a room covered in sunny yellow wainscoting. The symmetrical placement of the towel hooks and antique wall sconces around the mirror and shelf give the large sink even more presence and make it the focus of the room.

**Warm and cool.** Oranges, yellows, and other colors with a red tone impart a feeling of warmth to a room, but they also contract space. Cool colors—blues, greens, and colors with a blue tone—make a room seem larger. A light, monochromatic color scheme, one that uses different shades of one color, is restful and serene. Contrasting colors add vibrancy and excitement to a design. But a color scheme with contrasting colors can be overpowering unless the tones of the colors are varied. Note, too, that the temperature and intensity of colors will be affected by lighting.

**Contrast.** Light colors reflect light, making walls recede; thus, a small bathroom treated with light colors appears more spacious. Dark colors absorb light and can visually lower a ceiling or shorten a narrow room.

When considering colors for a small bathroom, remember that too much contrast has the same effect as a dark color: it reduces the sense of spaciousness. Contrasting colors work well for adding accents or drawing attention to interesting structural elements. But if you need to conceal a problem feature, it's best to use one color throughout the area.

## ADDING INTEREST WITH TEXTURE AND PATTERN

Texture and pattern work like color in defining a room's style and sense of space. The bathroom's surface materials may include many different textures, from a glossy countertop to smooth wood cabinets to a roughly surfaced quarry-tile floor.

Rough textures absorb light, make colors look duller, and lend a feeling of informality. Smooth textures reflect light and tend to suggest elegance or modernity. Using similar textures helps unify a design and create a mood.

Pattern choices should harmonize with the predominant style of the room. Though pattern is usually associated with wall coverings or a cabinet finish, even

natural substances such as wood and stone have patterns. While variation adds interest, too much variety can be overstimulating. It's best to let a strong feature or dominant pattern be the focus of your design and choose other surfaces to complement rather than compete with it.

Fabrics used in shower curtains, window treatments, and area rugs provide another opportunity to add texture and pattern. They also absorb sound and soften the look, important in a room with many hard surfaces.

## CREATING A DESIGN BOARD

Before you commit to any design decisions, you will want to live with them. Create a design board, placing swatches of fabric, paint, tile, laminate color chips, and any other such samples on a piece of posterboard. Hang it in your bathroom and live with it for a while. Some paint companies now have paint chips that are at least 9 by 12 inches, or you can paint an entire piece of posterboard in the colors that you contemplate using and live with them for a period of time.

Note, also, that the placement of light fixtures, and the kinds of bulbs used in them, will have an effect on the color. Make an effort to look at your design choices under the kind of light you have chosen. For details on lighting, see pages 48–49.

# Lighting design

Proper lighting in the bathroom enhances a beautifully decorated room and creates a safe and pleasant space. A good lighting plan provides shadowless, glarefree illumination for the entire room as well as bright, uniform light for specific tasks. The key to successful bathroom lighting is to use the right kinds of light, ambient and task, in the right combination.

## THE COLOR OF LIGHT

When deciding what kind of fixture or fixtures to install in your bathroom, you'll want to consider the color of light that different bulbs emit.

**Incandescent bulbs** have the warmest light, a pleasant reddish-yellow that makes skin tones look good and is comfortable to work under.

**Fluorescent tubes** emit a cooler blue or blue-white light. Formerly, fluorescent bulbs were criticized for their poor color rendition, giving off a somewhat greenish-blue light. Now the tubes are available in a variety of colors usually described as warm white, soft white, and daylight. However, the light is still cooler than that of incandescents.

**Halogen bulbs** emit the whitest light, closest to natural sunlight.

## THREE KINDS OF LIGHTING

Designers describe three specific kinds of lighting: ambient, task, and accent.

**Ambient or general lighting** fills a room with a soft level of light; it's usually the light you turn on when you walk into the room. How much light you need will depend on the colors of the cabinets, countertops, walls, and floor, as well as the size of the room. Dark colors absorb light; light colors reflect it.

**Task lighting** illuminates a particular area where you need to perform a task, such as putting on makeup or shaving, making the endeavor easier and safer.

**Accent lighting,** primarily decorative, is used to highlight an architectural feature, set a mood, or provide drama. Accent lights placed on top of a cabinet directed at the ceiling or in the toe-kick area under the cabinet can serve as night-lights.

## LIGHT FIXTURES

There are many choices for bathroom lighting. In a large bathroom, a separate fixture to light the shower or bath area may be needed.

**Recessed downlights,** or cans, are very popular and the least obtrusive fixture for general lighting. Available as small as 4 to 6 inches in width, they look like small circles in the ceiling. For

**Two wall sconces,** great lighting for applying makeup, are reflected in the full mirror behind the sink, effectively doubling the amount of light at the sink. Matching sconces are on the opposite wall.

best illumination, position these lights close enough together so their light patterns overlap.

**Surface-mounted lights** work well, especially in bathrooms than cannot accommodate recessed fixtures. Available in many styles and sizes, there are fixtures for either incandescent or fluorescent bulbs.

**Pendant lights,** lights that hang down, can work in a bathroom, either as the center light fixture in the ceiling for ambient light or placed over the vanity mirror for task lighting. Make sure the fixture is placed high enough so no one bumps into it.

**Shower fixtures** should be waterproof units fitted with neoprene seals.

**Vanity fixtures,** those around a makeup or shaving mirror, should spread light over a person's face rather than onto the mirror surface. To avoid heavy shadows, place lights on the sides of the mirror, not just overhead.

**Wall sconces** placed on either side of a mirror not only provide task lighting but offer an opportunity to make a design statement.

## DIMMERS

Dimmers, also called rheostats, enable you to set a fixture at any level of light from a soft glow for taking a bath to a radiant brightness for applying makeup, thus allowing for a variety of moods in the bathroom. Dimmers are also energy savers. It's easy and inexpensive to install a dimmer for incandescent bulbs. The initial cost of dimmers for fluorescents is higher and the variety of fixtures is limited. Dimmers can be round knobs that rotate or a toggle switch or slide bar that moves up and down.

# Lightbulbs and tubes

## INCANDESCENT

Incandescent light, the kind used most often in our homes, is produced by a tungsten thread that burns slowly inside a glass bulb. A-bulbs are traditional, R and PAR produce a more controlled beam, silvered bulbs diffuse light.

Low-voltage incandescent fixtures make good accent lighting. Operating on 12 or 24 volts, these lights require transformers, which are sometimes built in to the fixtures, to step down the voltage from standard 120-volt household circuits. Low-voltage fixtures are relatively expensive to buy but energy- and cost-efficient in the long run.

## FLUORESCENT

Fluorescent tubes, unrivaled for energy efficiency and lasting far longer than incandescent bulbs, are sometimes required by building codes for new kitchens. Older fluorescent tubes were slow to start, noisy, flickered, and had poor color rendition. Newer tubes with rapid-start features, electronic ballasts, and better fixture shielding for noise and flicker, come in a wide spectrum of colors. New subcompact tubes can be used in fixtures that usually require incandescent bulbs.

## HALOGEN

Quartz halogen lights are bright white light good for task and accent lighting. Halogen is usually low voltage but may use standard line current. The popular MR-16 bulb creates the tightest beam, while the PAR-36 bulb has a longer reach and wider coverage.

Halogen has two disadvantages: its high initial cost and its very high heat. Be sure to choose a fixture specifically designed for halogen bulbs.

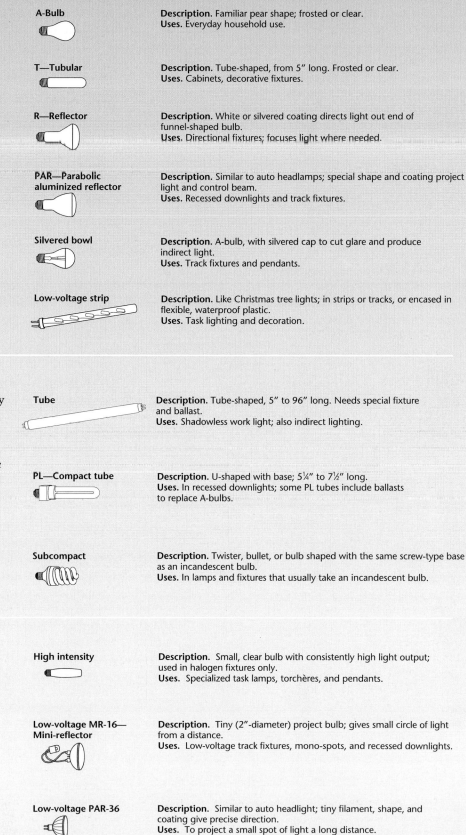

**A-Bulb**
**Description.** Familiar pear shape; frosted or clear.
**Uses.** Everyday household use.

**T—Tubular**
**Description.** Tube-shaped, from 5" long. Frosted or clear.
**Uses.** Cabinets, decorative fixtures.

**R—Reflector**
**Description.** White or silvered coating directs light out end of funnel-shaped bulb.
**Uses.** Directional fixtures; focuses light where needed.

**PAR—Parabolic aluminized reflector**
**Description.** Similar to auto headlamps; special shape and coating project light and control beam.
**Uses.** Recessed downlights and track fixtures.

**Silvered bowl**
**Description.** A-bulb, with silvered cap to cut glare and produce indirect light.
**Uses.** Track fixtures and pendants.

**Low-voltage strip**
**Description.** Like Christmas tree lights; in strips or tracks, or encased in flexible, waterproof plastic.
**Uses.** Task lighting and decoration.

**Tube**
**Description.** Tube-shaped, 5" to 96" long. Needs special fixture and ballast.
**Uses.** Shadowless work light; also indirect lighting.

**PL—Compact tube**
**Description.** U-shaped with base; 5¼" to 7½" long.
**Uses.** In recessed downlights; some PL tubes include ballasts to replace A-bulbs.

**Subcompact**
**Description.** Twister, bullet, or bulb shaped with the same screw-type base as an incandescent bulb.
**Uses.** In lamps and fixtures that usually take an incandescent bulb.

**High intensity**
**Description.** Small, clear bulb with consistently high light output; used in halogen fixtures only.
**Uses.** Specialized task lamps, torchères, and pendants.

**Low-voltage MR-16— Mini-reflector**
**Description.** Tiny (2"-diameter) project bulb; gives small circle of light from a distance.
**Uses.** Low-voltage track fixtures, mono-spots, and recessed downlights.

**Low-voltage PAR-36**
**Description.** Similar to auto headlight; tiny filament, shape, and coating give precise direction.
**Uses.** To project a small spot of light a long distance.

All of us are young once, most of us become old, and any of us can become disabled at any time. And as we age, our capabilities change. A bathroom design that considers the needs of all people who will use it—children, the elderly, and handicapped people—is called a universal design.

Universal design accommodates a wide range of individual preferences and abilities, and is most successful when it can be used efficiently and comfortably without great effort, when it minimizes hazards, and when it incorporates user-friendly materials.

## BARRIER-FREE FIXTURES

To create a more accessible bathroom you can adapt existing fixtures by adding grab bars and other devices or replace them altogether with fixtures specially designed for people with limited mobility. The National Kitchen and Bath Association (NKBA) and the Americans with Disabilities Act (ADA) of 1990 have set standards for fixtures and their placement. They recommend a clear floor space at least 30 by 48 inches in front of each fixture, although the spaces for individual fixtures may overlap. The following are their recommendations for fixtures.

### GUIDELINES FOR BARRIER-FREE BATHROOMS

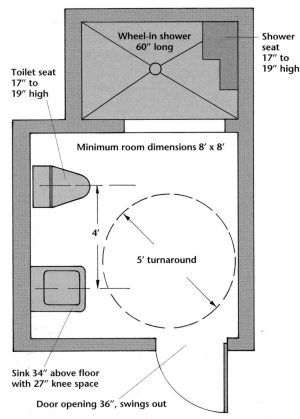

**These suggested clearances** allow enough space for people in wheelchairs to negotiate around the bathroom and to use all the fixtures.

**Showers.** There are two types of showers. One contains a seat and grab bars as well as handholds, soap holders, and adjustable, hand-held shower heads. A person in a wheelchair transfers from the chair to the shower seat. Ideally, the shower should be at least 42 inches square, although a 36-inch-square shower may work. The second type, at least 60 inches long, allows a person in a wheelchair to wheel in and shower while sitting in the wheelchair.

**Tubs.** Tubs must be equipped with a movable seat and have two parallel grab bars attached 33 to 36 inches above the floor.

**Sinks.** To be accessible to a wheelchair, a sink must have 27 inches of knee space below and project out far enough for a person to reach the faucets. It should be mounted 34 inches above the floor.

**Toilets.** Toilets with a higher seat, 17 to 19 inches off the floor rather than the standard 14 inches, are more comfortable. Standard toilets can be fitted with a thick, portable seat extension. Grab bars must be attached to the back wall and along one side of the toilet.

## ADDITIONAL GUIDELINES

Many of the general recommendations for bathroom heights and clearances (see pages 42–43) now reflect universal guidelines, but there are some things to consider. Some of the following accommodations for a universal bathroom have to do with the placement of the bathroom fixtures, others with their design.

- Doorways at least 32 inches wide, but 36 inches is preferable
- A center space of 60 by 60 inches for a turnaround
- Storage items placed 15 to 48 inches off the floor (or approximately knee to shoulder height)
- Light switches, electrical outlets, and thermostats no higher than 40 to 42 inches off the floor
- Rounded corners on counters
- Any glass in a tub/shower or partition should be laminated glass, tempered glass, or specially approved plastic
- A ventilation system with a fan that will exchange the air at least 8 times per hour (see page 81)
- Pressure-balanced or antiscald device for sink as well as tub and shower faucets
- Faucets with paddle-style handles
- Door handles, faucet handles, and cabinet hardware replaced with levers and pulls that can be operated with one hand
- Slip-resistant flooring
- Lighting fixtures placed out of the reach of a person seated or standing in a tub or shower

Once you have worked out an efficient layout, planned your storage requirements, and decided on color and lighting schemes, you can make your final decisions regarding new fixtures, vanity, flooring, and wall coverings (for help, see pages 54–63).

You can then decide on finishing touches, draw a new floor plan, order materials, set up a schedule for the work, review your insurance policies, and find out about building codes and permits before you begin the work.

## FINISHING TOUCHES

Finishing touches make the difference in any room and deserve careful attention. This is the time to choose all the hardware for the vanity and other storage units— doorknobs and drawer pulls as well as any moldings, curtains, and blinds. All these details help pull the design together and make a statement.

## DRAWING A NEW FLOOR PLAN

Draw your new floor plan, or working drawing, the same way you did the existing plan with paper and a ruler or using a kitchen design software program for your computer (see pages 38–39). On the new plan, include existing features you want to preserve and all the changes you're planning to make. If you prefer, you can hire a designer, drafter, or contractor to draw the final plan for you.

For more complicated projects, your local building department may require additional or more detailed drawings of structural, plumbing, and wiring changes. You may also need to show areas adjacent to the bathroom so building officials can determine how the project will affect the rest of your house. Elevation sketches are not required, but they will be helpful in planning the work.

## ORDERING MATERIALS

If you do the ordering of materials for your remodeling project, you'll need to compile a detailed master list. Not only will this launch your work, but it will also help you keep track of purchases and deliveries. For each item, specify the following information: name and model or serial number, manufacturer, source of material, date of order, expected delivery date, color,

**The finishing flourish** in this traditional bathroom is the mural wallpaper applied above the white tile walls. The outdoor scene surrounds the interesting window and creates a relationship between the vista on the wallpaper and the real trees immediately outside the window.

size or dimensions, quantity, price (including taxes and delivery charge), and a second choice just in case one is needed.

Ordering materials will also help you set up a schedule for the project. And this is a good time to review insurance policies to see what aspects of the job are covered, as well as to check the final plan against your budget.

## OBTAINING BUILDING PERMITS

To discover which building codes may affect your remodeling project and whether a building permit is required, check with your city or county building department.

You may need to apply for one or more permits: structural, plumbing, mechanical, heating or cooling, reroofing, or electrical. More complicated projects sometimes require that the design and working drawings be executed by an architect, designer, or state-licensed contractor.

For your permit you'll be charged either a flat fee or a percentage of the estimated cost of materials and labor. You may also have to pay a fee to have someone check the plans.

If you're acting as your own contractor, it's your responsibility to ask the building department to inspect the work as it progresses. Otherwise, a professional contractor will handle these inspections for you. The number of inspections depends on the complexity of the job. Failure to obtain a permit or an inspection may result in your having to dismantle completed work, so this is not something you can ignore.

# Working with professionals

Major bathroom remodeling projects are not easy work, so the first thing you want to do is evaluate your do-it-yourself skills. If you know how to draw plans but dislike physical labor, you'll need someone to perform the actual construction. If you like construction but can't draw, you can hire a professional to prepare working drawings. Or you can let professionals handle all the tasks, from drawing plans through applying the finishing touches.

Hiring the right professional for the job need not be daunting. No matter whom you consult, be as precise as possible about what you want. Collect photographs from magazines, brochures, and advertisements. Describe exactly what materials you want to use. Provide a preliminary plan and an idea of your budget. Write down questions you have as you think of them. The more information you can supply, the better job a professional will be able to do for you.

A bathroom remodel is more than just a construction project; it's a personal project, a reflection of your home and family. In choosing a professional, look for someone who is not only technically and artistically skilled but also someone with whom you and your family feel totally comfortable.

## ARCHITECT OR DESIGNER?

Either an architect or a designer can draw plans acceptable to building department officials; each can send out bids, help you select a contractor, and supervise the contractor's performance to ensure that your plans and time schedule are being followed. Some architects and designers even double as their own contractors.

Most states do not require designers to be licensed, as architects must be; designers may charge less for their labor. Architects can do stress calculations if these are needed; designers need state-licensed engineers to design the structure and sign the working drawings.

Bathroom designers are specially trained and know about the latest building materials and techniques. An interior designer specializes in decorating and furnishing of rooms and can be hired for the finishing touches. They both can suggest fresh, innovative ideas and offer advice. Through their contacts you have access to materials not available at the retail level.

Architects and designers may or may not charge for time spent in an exploratory interview. For plans you'll probably be charged on an hourly basis. If an architect or designer selects the contractor and keeps an eye on

**Steps leading up** to this whirlpool bathtub give it a real presence in the room. Elegant touches include a canvas balloon shade whose fabric folds mimic the texture of the wallpaper and a gold-framed mirror that echoes the gold faucets. A pendant light fixture over the whirlpool tub has matching wall sconces on either side of the pedestal sink.

construction, plan to pay either an hourly rate or a percentage of the cost of materials and labor—usually 15 to 25 percent. State a description of the services and amount of the charges in advance in writing to prevent later expensive misunderstandings.

## CHOOSING A CONTRACTOR

Contractors do more than construction. Often they can draw plans acceptable to building department officials and can obtain building permits. A contractor's experience and technical know-how may end up saving you money.

To find a contractor, ask architects, designers, and friends for recommendations. Compare bids from at least three state-licensed contractors, giving each one either an exact description and sketches of the desired remodeling or plans and specifications prepared by an architect or designer. Include a detailed account of who will be responsible for what work.

Don't make your decision on price alone; reliability, quality of work, and on-time performance are also important. Ask contractors for the names and phone numbers of their clients. Call several and ask them about the contractor's performance and then inspect the work, both a finished project and one in progress, if possible. Check bank and credit references to determine the contractor's financial responsibility. Make sure the contractor has insurance. Don't hire someone who rushes to talk about payment before any work is done, is hesitant to give references, or is late. The relationship of contractor and client is crucial to a successful project. Both must understand the other's needs, be open to communication, and, most of all, trust each other. Good rapport is important to a successful job.

Though some contractors may want a fee based on a percentage of the cost of materials and labor, it's usually wiser to insist on a fixed-price bid. This protects you against both a rise in the cost of materials (assuming that the contractor does the buying) and the chance that the work will take more time, adding to your labor costs. Many states limit the amount of "good faith" money that contractors can require before work begins. And don't underestimate the time it will take to do the work.

## HIRING SUBCONTRACTORS

When you act as your own general contractor and put various parts of your project out to bid with a variety of subcontractors, you must use the same care you'd exercise in hiring a general contractor.

You'll need to check references, financial resources, and insurance coverage of a number of subcontractors. Once you've received bids and made your choices, work out a detailed contract for each specific job and carefully supervise all the work.

## Who's Who

Many of the professionals involved with home remodeling belong to organizations that certify licenses in the field. These organizations can answer questions and provide information to the homeowner.

### AIA—The American Institute of Architects

This is the national professional organization for licensed (by the state) architects.
1735 New York Ave.
Washington, DC 20006
(202) 626-7300
www.aiaonline.com

### AIBD—American Institute of Building Design

Award is Professional Building Designer (PBD).
991 Post Rd. East
Westport, CT 06880
(800) 366-2423 or (203) 227-3640
www.aibd.org

### ASID—The American Society of Interior Designers

Membership is based on education, experience, and testing by the National Council for Interior Design Qualifications.
608 Massachusetts Ave. NE
Washington, DC 20002
(202) 546-3480
www.asid.org

### NAHB—National Association of Home Builders

Certifies educational and managerial standards. Award is Certified Graduate Remodeler (CGR).
1201 15th St. NW
Washington, DC 20005
(800) 368-5242, ext. 216, or (202) 822-0216
www.nahb.com

### NARI—National Association of the Remodeling Industry

Award is Certified Remodeler (CR).
4900 Seminary Rd., Suite 320
Alexandria, VA 22311
(703) 575-1100
www.nari.org

### NKBA—National Kitchen & Bath Association

Qualified professionals are Certified Bathroom Designers (CBD).
687 Willow Grove St.
Hackettstown, NJ 07840
(800) 367-6522 or (908) 852-0033
www.nkba.com

# Cabinets

Storage plays an important role in bathroom design. The traditional storage units are a medicine cabinet in the wall above the sink and a base cabinet with a countertop and sink on top forming a vanity. But bath storage areas can be more stylish, with mirrors, sink, lighting, and backsplash treatment integrated into the design. You could add a bank of wall cabinets, have built-in units between areas of use, or plan a floor-to-ceiling unit in a narrow space. If you don't find what you're looking for in the bath department, you can take a look at kitchen units in the kitchen department.

**Cabinet construction.** The durability of a cabinet depends on the type and thickness of the materials used and the quality of construction. The two basic cabinet construction styles are face frame and frameless. Traditional American cabinets mask the raw front edges of each box with a 1 by 2-inch face frame. On European, or frameless, cabinets, a simple narrow trim strip covers raw edges; doors and drawers usually fit to within ¼ inch of each other, revealing a thin sliver of the trim. Door hinges are invisible. Most are built with columns of holes drilled every 32 millimeters on the inside frame so that interchangeable components will fit together, making frameless cabinets versatile. Frameless cabinets allow for better access and so increase storage space.

**Purchasing cabinets.** You can buy ready-to-assemble kits, stock, custom, or modular cabinets. Ready-to-assemble kits (RTA) come with all the parts and hardware and cost the least, because you assemble them yourself using a screwdriver or wrench. They offer the fewest design choices. Mass-produced, standard-size stock units are the least expensive option for ready-made cabinets and can be an excellent choice if you clearly understand your needs. Though it's generally a more expensive approach, custom shops can match old cabinets, build to odd configurations, and accommodate details that cannot be handled by stock cabinets. A new hybrid, the custom modular cabinet, is manufactured but offers more design flexibility than stock. Not surprisingly, modular cabinets cost more, too; you place an order and wait.

**Standard sizes.** You can purchase a vanity cabinet with or without a countertop and sink. Some manufacturers produce modular cabinet and shelf units for use with their vanities; other units include laundry bins, medicine cabinets, and closets. Standard width is 30 inches, increasing at 3- or 6-inch intervals, but some are as narrow as 12 inches and as wide as 60 inches. Standard height is 32 inches but can range from 28 to 36 inches; standard depth is 21 inches but can range up to 24 inches.

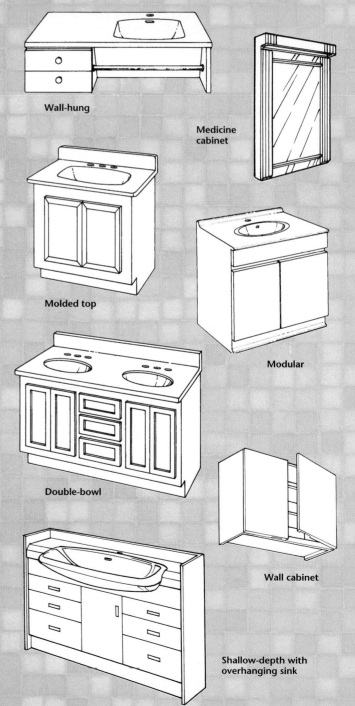

Wall-hung

Medicine cabinet

Molded top

Modular

Double-bowl

Wall cabinet

Shallow-depth with overhanging sink

# Countertops

Choosing a countertop is a matter of balancing the look of the material with its practicality. Any of the six surfaces described below can be installed in a bathroom. Think about edge treatments that can dress up a counter, such as a bullnose edge, a wood strip, or inlays in a solid surface.

## STONE

Granite and marble are beautiful natural materials for countertops. Solid stone slabs are very expensive; stone tiles, including slate and limestone, are less expensive alternatives. With stone other than granite, look into the latest sealers.
**Pros.** Stone is very strong and durable, water resistant, and easy to clean.
**Cons.** Stone is heavy and requires a strong base; it must be custom installed. Oil, alcohol, and any acid (even chemicals in some water supplies) will stain marble or damage its high-gloss finish; granite can stand up to all of these.

## PLASTIC LAMINATE

Composed of resin-impregnated paper bonded to a particleboard core, laminate comes in a wide range of colors, textures, and patterns. Ready-made molded tops called post-formed are the least expensive option.
**Pros.** Durable, easy to clean, water resistant, and relatively inexpensive.
**Cons.** It can scratch, scorch, and chip. High-gloss surfaces show dirt and water marks. The dark backing shows at its seams.

## SOLID SURFACE

Made from polyester or acrylic resins and mineral fillers, this smooth material is manufactured in sheets ½ inch thick that can be formed into seamless designs (with an integral sink, if desired).
**Pros.** Durable, water resistant, nonporous, and easy to clean, it resists bacteria and mold. Blemishes and scratches can be sanded out.
**Cons.** Easily scratched, expensive, needs firm support from below, and usually requires professional installation.

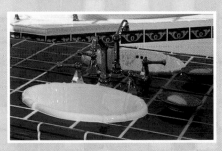

## SYNTHETIC MARBLE

A group of man-made products, called collectively "cast polymers," includes cultured marble, cultured onyx, and cultured granite. Quality can vary, so look for certification from the International Cast Polymer Association (ICPA) or the International Association of Plumbing and Mechanical Officials (IAPMO).
**Pros.** Waterproof, easy to clean, and relatively inexpensive. Countertops are available with integrated sinks.
**Cons.** Not very durable. Scratches and dings are hard to mend because the surface is often only a thin veneer.

## CERAMIC TILE

Good-looking ceramic tile comes in many colors, textures, and patterns. It is formed by pressing clay under pressure to shape it, then it is dried and fired in a kiln, where it hardens. Tiles can be glazed or unglazed, but nonporous glazed tiles won't soak up spills and stains.
**Pros.** Installed correctly, ceramic tile is scratch resistant, water resistant, and long lasting.
**Cons.** Grout is hard to keep clean, even when a grout sealer is used (using thin grout spaces helps). The hard surface can chip glass containers. High-gloss tiles show every smudge.

## WOOD

Butcher block, a popular ready-made top, is a generic term for edge-grain or end-grain maple or oak that's cut in strips and laminated together. Edge-joined oak, redwood, sugar pine, and teak are also used for counters. In areas that will get wet (which includes most bathroom surfaces), it must be protected on all sides with a good sealer like polyurethane.
**Pros.** Warm, handsome, natural, and easily installed.
**Cons.** Wood can scratch and dent, and it must be sealed with polyurethane in the bathroom.

# Sinks

Sinks come in so many shapes, sizes, colors, materials, and styles that there is a choice for every taste and budget. The selection of sink materials includes vitreous china, fiberglass-reinforced plastic, enameled cast iron, enameled steel, solid surfacing, composites like cast polymer, stainless steel, and even glass. Brass and copper sinks make striking accents but require zealous maintenance. The newest styles include above-the-counter bowls, overhanging bowls, and sculptural pedestal sinks that look like works of art.

Sinks have either no holes for fittings or holes for 4, 6, or 8-inch faucet assemblies; some also have holes for spray attachments.

**Deck mounted.** Set into a hole in the countertop of the vanity, these sinks are the most popular type. They are available in a wide selection of materials and can be mounted in a number of ways. A self-rimmed sink has a molded overlap that's supported by the edge of the countertop cutout. A rimmed sink has a flat rim with surrounding metal strips to hold the basin to the countertop. An undermounted sink is recessed beneath the countertop opening and held in place by metal clips.

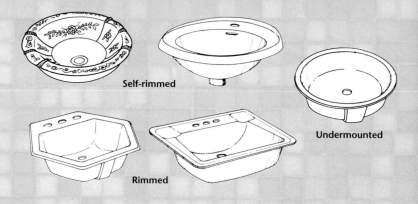

Self-rimmed

Undermounted

Rimmed

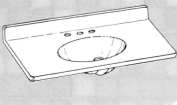

**Integral.** Made of solid-surface material, synthetic marble, or fiberglass, an integral sink and countertop has no joints, so installation and cleaning are easy. This one-piece molded unit sits on top of a vanity. Sink color can either match the countertop or complement it; edge banding and other border options are available. It also comes with double-bowl units.

**Pedestal.** Typically made of vitreous china in a wide range of traditional and modern designs, these elegant sinks are easy to install. The pedestal usually hides the plumbing. Some models have old-style vanity legs. Pedestal sinks are generally among the highest-priced basins and are a good choice only in rooms that don't require storage space beneath the sink.

**Wall hung.** Materials and styling of these sinks is similar to pedestals; in fact, some designs are available in either version. Some styles include an overhanging bowl. Generally the least expensive and most compact sink choice, they are relatively easy to install. Wall-hung units are supported by hangers or angle brackets. If you're installing a wall-hung sink for the first time, plan to tear out part of the wall to add a support ledger.

**Console.** Freestanding sinks with two or four legs. Two-leg sinks are bolted to the wall. Console sinks are similar in look to pedestal sinks but with a wider deck for storing soap and other necessities. Some versions include a storage shelf or rack below.

# Bathtubs

Bathtub selection is no longer limited to the white 30 by 60-inch bathtub that once dominated the 5- by 7-foot bathroom. New and more comfortable tub shapes and sizes are available in an array of materials and colors. Materials include enameled steel, which is relatively inexpensive and lighter in weight than cast iron but noisy, cold, and prone to chipping; enameled cast iron, which is durable and warmer to the touch but very heavy; fiberglass, which is economical, lightweight, and easily installed but can scratch and show wear after 10 to 15 years; and acrylic, which is durable, less prone to scratching because the color is solid throughout, able to be molded into shapes, and lightweight.

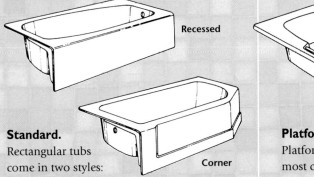

Recessed

Corner

**Standard.**
Rectangular tubs come in two styles: recessed and corner. Recessed tubs fit between two side walls and against a back wall and have a finished front apron. Corner models have one finished side and end and may be right- or left-handed. If space allows, choose a model longer, up to 72 inches, and deeper, 16 inches rather than the standard 14 inches, for greater comfort.

Also if space permits, there is a corner model with the tub positioned at an angle.

**Platform or sunken.**
Platform or sunken tubs, most commonly available in enameled cast iron or acrylic, are either set in a raised platform or sunk in the floor. Extra framing is often needed, especially for installation on an upper floor. Interior shapes and features vary. Built-in headrests, armrests, seating shelves, and grab bars are available.

**Freestanding.** An old-fashioned freestanding tub, such as the classic clawfoot model, is often a focal point in a traditional design. You can buy reproductions or a reconditioned original. Such tubs can also serve as showers with the installation of a Victorian-inspired shower head diverter and curtain rod hardware.

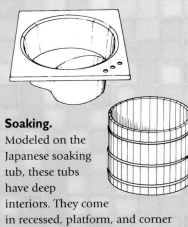

**Soaking.**
Modeled on the Japanese soaking tub, these tubs have deep interiors. They come in recessed, platform, and corner models, with rectangular or round interiors of fiberglass or acrylic.

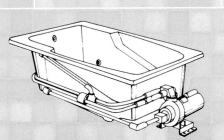

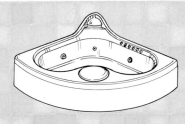

**Whirlpool.** Usually made of fiberglass-reinforced acrylic, these tubs come in a variety of shapes from rectangular to round to oval to an hourglass shape with controls along the side. Whirlpool tubs contain a pump, ranging from ½ to 3 horsepower, that circulates water and air through jets. The pump is located under or near the tub and should be accessible through an access panel at the side, front, or rear of the tub. The number and design of the jets may vary from a few strong jets to many softer outlets. The best models have jets that are adjustable for water volume, air–water mixture, and direction. These tubs may require an extra-capacity water heater or separate in-line heater. Because of their extra weight, whirlpools may need extra floor framing.

# Showers

Showers are a vital part of a bathroom. The choices for creating a shower include using a prefabricated kit, matching separate components, or building the shower from scratch. You can add amenities like multiple shower heads, a hand-held shower head, spray bars, a bench or fold-down seat, a shelf for supplies, and grab bars.

You can mix and match shower base, surround, and doors to create your own design; choose a shower or tub/shower kit that comes with overlapping wall panels, adhesive, and caulking; use a shower or tub/shower wall kit with an existing shower base or tub; or add shower or tub/shower doors that you can buy separately. Because of their size, one-piece molded shower or tub/shower surrounds are used primarily in new homes or additions; if you have oversize doors in your house, you may be able to use one of these units.

Size is important; make sure you carefully measure the installation area and the unit before you buy. Units are available in fiberglass-reinforced plastic, acrylic, plastic laminate, and synthetic marble.

**Shower surrounds.** Most shower surrounds require framing for support; you fasten the panel flanges to the framing. The shower base, walls, and door can be purchased individually or in a kit. Some models come with ceilings. For comfort, choose a shower that's at least 36 inches square. The height varies, but 84 inches is common. Corner and circular shower models are available. Circular showers have doors that double as walls.

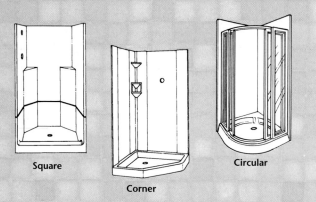

Square

Corner

Circular

**Tub/shower surrounds.**
Tub/shower surrounds must also have framing for support. You can purchase the tub, walls, and door in a kit, or buy a separate recessed tub and match it with compatible prefabricated wall panels, a molded one-piece surround, or a custom wall treatment (such as tile panels). Molded fiberglass wall panels or one-piece surrounds may include molded soap dishes, ledges, and grab bars.

You can also add a shower head or install a hand-held shower attachment to convert an existing tub surround to a tub/shower. Shower attachments are mounted to the wall or tub spout.

Separate panels

One-piece

**Shower bases.** Purchased separately or in a kit, a shower base can be made of fiberglass, acrylic, terrazzo (a concrete/stone mix), cast polymer, or a solid-surface material and comes in standard sizes in rectangular, square, or corner shapes. All come with a hole drilled for the drain. You can match a base to a tub or other fixture because many manufacturers make both.

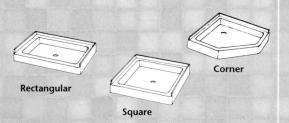

Rectangular

Corner

Square

**Shower doors.** Available in a variety of styles, shower doors are typically made of tempered safety glass with aluminum frames, which come in many finishes. The glazing can be clear or, for added privacy, textured or tinted. Tub/showers usually have sliding doors, often with towel bars. Swinging, folding, and pivot doors (not shown) can be installed with right or left openings. Folding doors are made of rigid plastic panels or flexible plastic sheeting. Frameless glass panels with the appropriate hardware can be used as shower doors or wall panels.

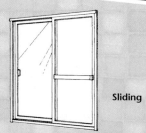

Swinging

Folding

Sliding

# Fittings for fixtures

Fittings, sold separately from fixtures, need to be durable and easy to use. The best ones are made of brass and come in several finishes, including chrome, pewter, gold, and brightly colored enamel. Ceramic or nylon-disk designs are easier to maintain than older systems that use washers.

Sink fittings come in three basic types: single, center-set, and spread-fit controls. A single-control fitting has a combined faucet and lever or knob that controls water flow and temperature. A center-set control has separate hot and cold water controls and a faucet, all mounted on a base. A spread-fit control has separate hot and cold water controls and a faucet,

each mounted independently. The number of holes in the sink and the distances between them—4, 6, or 8 inches—determine which fittings can be used. If fittings are to be attached to the wall or counter, the holes can be placed to suit the fittings.

In addition to the controls, tubs require a spout and drain. Tub/showers need a spout, shower head, diverter valve, and drain. By law, new shower heads can deliver only 2.5 gallons of water per minute, but you can install as many shower heads as you like. Single-control fittings are available with pressure balancing and temperature-limiting valves (see page 45).

Two things to consider: When looking at the design of fittings, imagine how well you could work the controls with soapy hands and how easy they are to clean.

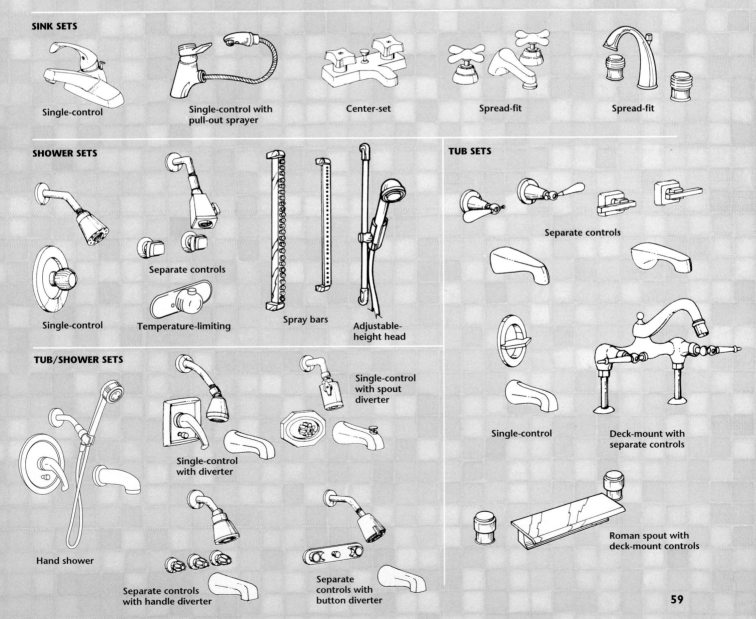

## SINK SETS

Single-control

Single-control with pull-out sprayer

Center-set

Spread-fit

Spread-fit

## SHOWER SETS

Single-control

Separate controls

Temperature-limiting

Spray bars

Adjustable-height head

## TUB SETS

Separate controls

Single-control

Deck-mount with separate controls

Roman spout with deck-mount controls

## TUB/SHOWER SETS

Hand shower

Single-control with diverter

Single-control with spout diverter

Separate controls with handle diverter

Separate controls with button diverter

# Toilets and bidets

In 1994, with an eye toward water conservation the U.S. government enacted national standards that limit the water use of residential toilets to 1.6 gallons or less per flush. Ultra-low-flush (ULF) toilets are now required in all new construction.

Toilets have one of three types of flushing mechanisms: gravity fed, pressure assisted, or electric. Gravity fed relies on the force of the water released from the tank into the bowl to flush waste down the drain. With less water per flush, some models have narrower bowls, a wider drainpipe, and a shorter trapway to aid in flushing. Pressure-assisted toilets use a tank of compressed air to force the water through the bowl and out the trap. An electric pump on some models helps push the water and waste through the toilet. It is much quieter than the other types.

Vitreous china, a particularly hard china that's impervious to water, is still the best material for toilets, but new styling, new colors, and new technologies are updating the standard model. In addition to traditional and antique models, toilets now come in sleek European designs, standard or low-profile heights, and rounded or elongated bowl shapes.

**One-piece.** One-piece toilets, European in design, are characterized by their low profile, usually 19 to 26 inches high at the tank. These units are designed for floor and wall mounting and are available with round or elongated bowls. Their design and efficient look make them easier to clean and, with their easy installation, make them a popular choice.

**Two-piece.** The most common style, two-piece toilets come in many models and can be mounted on the floor or on the wall. A wall-hung toilet offers better access for a person in a wheelchair and makes floor cleaning easier. If you don't already have a wall-hung toilet, you'll face fairly major alterations to the wall framing and the floor. In a period reproduction, the tank is mounted on the wall high above the bowl.

If you have special needs, consider special toilet designs. The rim of a higher-seat safety toilet is 17 to 19 inches above the floor, compared to the 14- or 15-inch height of a conventional bowl. Or you can add a cushioned seat, made of vinyl-covered foam rubber to an existing seat. Safety bars are a must.

Wall tank

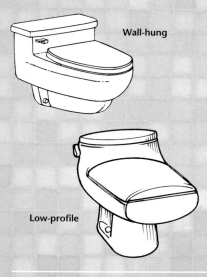

Wall-hung

Low-profile

Standard

Safety

## BIDETS

A must-have in Europe but only beginning to be popular here, a bidet is used primarily for personal hygiene. Best installed next to the toilet, it's floor mounted and plumbed with hot and cold water. Available with wall or deck-mounted water controls, a bidet comes with a spray spout or a vertical spray located in the center of the bowl. Some have rim jets for rinsing to maintain bowl cleanliness. Most models also have a pop-up stopper that allows the unit to double as a foot bath or laundry basin.

Spread-fit        Center-fit

# Heating and ventilation

For a comfortable bathroom, chilly air, steam, and excess heat have to be kept under control. You don't want to spoil the soothing effects of a hot bath by stepping out into a cool bathroom or find it difficult to shave because steam from the shower has not dissipated.

Electric heat can be provided by baseboard or wall panels. Or a small heater in the wall or ceiling may be all that you need to stay warm. Bathroom heaters warm rooms by two methods: convection and radiation. Convection heaters warm the air in a room, which then heats surfaces and objects that it contacts. Radiant heaters emit infrared or electromagnetic waves that warm the objects and surfaces without warming the intervening air. If you're installing a new slab or subfloor, you may want to consider radiant heating pipes below.

Most building codes require that bathrooms have either natural or forced ventilation. Forced ventilation is required in windowless bathrooms. Some codes specify that the exhaust fan must be on the same switch as the lights. But even if you have good natural ventilation, an exhaust fan can exchange the air in a bathroom faster than an open window; in bad weather, a fan can keep the elements out and still remove stale air.

**Electric heaters.** Wall- or ceiling-mounted convection heaters usually have an electrically heated resistance coil and a small fan to move the heated air. A heater placed in the toe-kick space under the vanity helps warm the floor. Radiant heaters using infrared light-bulbs may be surface mounted on the ceiling or recessed between joists. Radiant heating panels are generally flush mounted on a wall or ceiling. Electric heaters are easy to install and clean to operate.

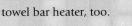

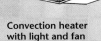

Radiant heater with heat lamps

Convection heater with light and fan

Radiant or convection wall heater

**Gas heaters.** There are heaters available for either propane or natural gas. Though most are convection heaters, there is one radiant type: a catalytic heater. Most gas heaters are flush mounted in a wall. Options include electric ignition and wall-mounted thermostats. All gas heaters require a supply line and must be vented to the outside.

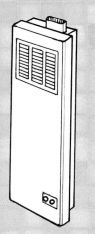

Convection wall heater

**Heated towel bars.** Besides gas and electricity, another heat source has reappeared on the bathroom scene: hot water. The original idea was to warm bath towels, but now these hydronic units—wall or floor mounted—are being billed as radiators as well. You can find electric versions of the towel bar heater, too.

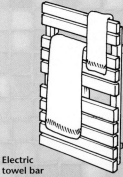
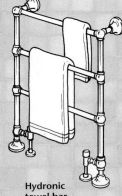

Electric towel bar

Hydronic towel bar

**Exhaust fans.** You can buy fans to mount in the wall or ceiling. Some models are combined with a light or a heater or both. Some fan/light combinations have the fan turn on every time the light is turned on; other models are motion sensitive and turn on when a person enters the room. The Home Ventilating Institute recommends that the fan be capable of exchanging the air at least eight times every hour (for details, see page 81). Most fans also have a noise rating measured in sones; the lower the number, the quieter the fan.

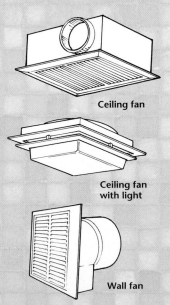

Ceiling fan

Ceiling fan with light

Wall fan

# Flooring

Bathroom floors have to be moisture resistant, durable, and easy to clean. The floor should also be appealing to you. In choosing, you will want to look at the characteristics of the various flooring materials—resilient, ceramic tile, wood, laminate, and stone—as well as consider the kind of subflooring you have or will need, and the total cost, including the material and the installation.

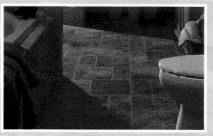

## WOOD

The three basic types of wood flooring are strip, narrow tongue-and-groove boards in random lengths; plank, tongue-and-groove boards in various widths and random lengths; and wood tile, often laid parquet-style. For durability, choose only hardwoods, not soft like pine or fir. For added durability finish with polyurethane.

**Pros.** Wood floors are warm, feel good underfoot, resist wear, and can be refinished. They often look better with age.

**Cons.** Moisture will damage wood floors, which is an important consideration in a bathroom. In addition, an adequate substructure is crucial. Polyurethane-finished floors can never be waxed, only buffed. Bleaching and some staining processes may wear unevenly and are difficult to repair.

## STONE

Natural stone, such as slate, flagstone, marble, granite, and limestone, has been used for centuries. With sealers and finishes, it is even more practical today. Stone can be used in its natural shape or cut in blocks or tiles. Irregular shapes, called flagstones, have grouted joints; squares are butted together.

**Pros.** Stone floors are easy to maintain and virtually indestructible.

**Cons.** Costly, cold, and slippery underfoot, although new textured surfaces are safer. Must be sealed and needs a strong, well-supported subfloor.

## LAMINATE

Like laminate countertops, laminate flooring is made of a layer of veneer with a protective coating bonded to a fiber-board core with a moisture-resistant backing. Available in many looks from wood to stone to tile. Use products recommended for use in the bathroom and follow installation instructions carefully to avoid moisture damage later.

**Pros.** Durable, easy to install, resistant to dents and stains, and easy to clean.

**Cons.** Use only products specifically recommended for bathrooms; moisture under the surface can swell the material.

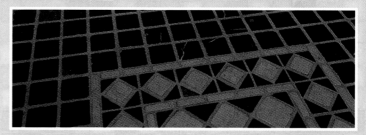

## RESILIENT

Made of vinyl, resilients come in square tiles and sheets up to 12 feet wide, eliminating the need for seams in most bathrooms. Available in two forms: inlaid, in which color is created with chips fused into the material in the manufacturing process; and rotogravure, in which the design is printed on the surface.

**Pros.** Comfortable to walk on, easy to care for, and affordable. Comes in a great variety of styles, colors, textures. Tiles are often easier to lay than large sheets.

**Cons.** Vulnerable to dents and scratches, especially in the more economic flooring. Must be installed on a very flat subfloor. Moisture can collect in the seams if tiles are not installed properly.

## CERAMIC TILE

Floor tiles are thicker and usually larger (at least 8 inches square) than tiles designed for walls. Tiles used on the floor include glazed ceramic tiles (preferably with a matte or textured finish for slip resistance) that are available in many colors, unglazed terra-cotta pavers, and unglazed quarry tiles made of a stonelike clay that needs to be sealed. A good floor choice if you are adding radiant floor heating.

**Pros.** Ceramic tile is very durable and easy to maintain. The many sizes and colors available can be creatively mixed to produce a wide range of treatments and designs.

**Cons.** Ceramic tile is hard on the feet because it has no "give," and it is noisy, cold, and, if glazed, slippery underfoot. Tiles can be costly and can chip or crack. Grouting can be difficult to keep clean and can come loose.

# Wallcoverings

Bathroom walls should be heat and moisture resistant, easy to clean, and able to withstand constant use. In the shower and tub-surround areas, ceramic tile is the logical choice. But in addition to those areas, your bathroom may include a good bit of wall space. Wall treatments in these areas, which also must be very durable, help define the overall look of your bath.

## CERAMIC TILE

Wall tiles, lighter and thinner than floor tiles, are glazed and offer great variety in color and design. Their relatively light weight is a plus for vertical installation. The glazed surface is water resistant, though the bodies are porous.

Standard sizes for wall tiles range from 3- to 12-inch squares and include 4¼- by 8½-inch rectangles; thicknesses vary from ¼ to ⅜ inch. Other sizes and shapes are available. Many come with matching trim pieces for edges and corners.

Wall tiles are also available in pregrouted panels, a handy shortcut that reduces installation time and effort. Designed primarily for tub and shower areas, a panel contains up to 64 tiles, each measuring 4¼ inches square. The panels have flexible, water-repellent grout.

Colorful and versatile, mosaic tiles are small, generally 2 by 2 inches or less, and for this reason can be installed on curved surfaces. Mosaics come in sheets, with the tiles mounted on thread mesh or paper backing or joined with silicone rubber. Once they're in place, you grout these sheets like any other wall tiles.
**Pros.** Installed correctly, tile is durable, scratch resistant, and water resistant.
**Cons.** Grout is hard to keep clean, even when a grout sealer is used (using thin grout spaces helps). The hard surface can chip glass containers.

## STONE

Marble, slate, limestone, and granite, whether as 8- or 12-inch tiles or wider sheets, can be used in many of the same places in the bathroom as ceramic tile. Most stone, especially marble, should be thoroughly sealed for wall use; untreated, it can be stained or eaten away by acids in cleaning supplies or even by acids naturally found in household water.
**Pros.** Strong and durable, water resistant, and easy to clean, stone offers a natural and luxurious look.
**Cons.** Stone is very heavy and must be custom installed. It also stains easily (except for granite, which can stand up to all chemicals). Stone tiles can be expensive but, used as accents in the right place, they can go a long way.

## GLASS BLOCK

Glass blocks allow in ambient daylight and protect privacy at the same time. Available in 3- or 4-inch-thick square blocks in a variety of sizes and in rectangular blocks in a more limited selection. Textures can be smooth, wavy, rippled, bubbly, or crosshatched.
**Pros.** It can be used for an interior wall to define areas of use. A good insulator.
**Cons.** Expensive. Often requires extra support in the floor. Installing glass blocks with mortar is a job for a professional. Mortarless block systems make a simpler installation for do-it-yourselfers.

## WALLPAPER

A wallpaper for the bathroom should be scrubbable, durable, and stain resistant. Solid-vinyl wallpapers, which come in a wide variety of colors and textures, are the best choice. Many patterns are available; some replicate other surfaces such as linen; wallpaper borders add punch to ceiling lines and openings.
**Pros.** Warms up a room full of cold surfaces. Available in myriad colors, patterns, and textures.
**Cons.** Good ventilation is crucial for good upkeep. Wallpaper should not be used in windowless bathrooms or ones without good ventilation.

## WOOD

Tongue-and-groove wood paneling (natural, stained, bleached, or painted) provides a charming accent to country designs. Wainscoting is the most popular application; the paneling is separated from wallpaper or paint above it by a traditional chair rail.
**Pros.** Wood brings warmth to a bathroom. Moldings add a bit of style and a wide selection is available. Specialty shops will often custom match an old favorite to order.
**Cons.** Wood can be damaged by water and heat, so care must be taken when it is used near any fixtures.

# REMODELING BASICS

**Y**ou've decided it's time to remodel your bathroom—a decision that will involve considerable time and energy. After reviewing lots of bathroom ideas, you're ready to start. This chapter will help get you from the ideas to the reality. Here are some survival tips to help you keep the work going smoothly.

Know what you want before you begin. Will you give your bathroom a fresh look with new paint in a favorite color and strategically placed lighting? Or is this the time for a major remodel that involves installing a skylight, moving a wall to increase storage, and adding new fixtures?

Be safe. It's important to keep you and your family safe during a remodel. Clean up the area every day. Dispose of debris carefully. Wear protective gear and follow the manufacturers' instructions. If you need more detailed information about step-by-step procedures, take a look at the *Sunset* books *Basic Carpentry*, *Basic Plumbing*, and *Basic Wiring*, or consult a professional.

Be comfortable. You'll want to keep the bathroom usable for much of the renovation, especially if you have only one bathroom. Careful scheduling of each job is essential. It helps to designate one family member to deal with the contractor or other people you may hire. That way, mixed messages are less likely to happen.

Lastly, be as flexible as you can throughout the remodeling process. It may help to lessen the inconvenience by thinking about the pleasure of a new bathroom designed especially to meet your family's needs.

To be sufficiently prepared for a bathroom remodel, you will want to have a clear idea of the sequence of steps necessary to complete the job, obtain necessary permits, evaluate your own ability to perform the tasks, and have the proper materials and tools. One of the first decisions will be to determine whether you will do the work yourself or get professional help.

## ASSESS YOURSELF

Be realistic when assessing your do-it-yourself abilities. The skill level required for a bathroom remodel depends on what improvements you are making. Surface treatments—such as painting, wallpapering, or simply replacing light fixtures—can be accomplished by a homeowner with some do-it-yourself experience. Some projects may require specialized tools, usually available from a building supply or home improvement center.

Complex remodeling tasks—such as moving load-bearing walls, running new drain and vent pipes, or wiring new electrical circuits—are often best handled by professionals. Smaller jobs within these areas, though, are within the skills of an experienced homeowner.

Even if there's not much you can build, you may discover a talent for demolition—and save some money in the process. Some contractors may not want to relinquish this task. If you take it on, be sure you're finished by the time the remodeling crew is ready to begin.

## PLANNING YOUR PROJECT

Putting careful thought into your preparations can save you extra work and inconvenience later. The bigger your remodeling project, the greater the need for careful planning. If you have only one bathroom, your goal is to keep it in operating order as much of the time as possible. With careful scheduling, the remodeling time will be easier for the entire family.

Be sure to obtain any necessary permits from your local building department. A contractor, if you hire one, will do this job for you. But if you're doing the work yourself, you'll need to secure permits and arrange for inspections. Finally, before the work begins, check the suggestions below.

- Establish the sequence of jobs to be performed, and estimate the time required to complete each one.

- If you're hiring professional help, make sure you have legally binding contracts and schedules with contractors and subcontractors.

- If electricity, gas, or water must be shut off by the utility company, arrange for the cutoff date.

- Locate an area for temporarily storing fixtures or appliances.

- Measure fixtures for adequate clearance through doorways and up and down staircases.

If you're hiring help, a contractor's services include these steps:

- Locate a site for dumping refuse, and secure necessary permits.

- Obtain all required building permits.

- Arrange for timely delivery of materials and be sure you have all the necessary tools on hand.

## HOW TO USE THIS CHAPTER

Reading all sections of this chapter through quickly will help you to get a general feeling for what's involved in bathroom remodeling.

In the first three sections, you'll find an overview of the structural, plumbing, and electrical systems. Even if you don't plan to do the work yourself, you may want to review these sections for background information. Understanding basic systems enables you to plan more effectively and appreciate the reasons for code restrictions affecting your plans.

Many of your remodeling hours may be spent tearing out old work. To minimize the effort, we've included removal procedures along with installation instructions in the sections on fixtures, wallcoverings, flooring, and cabinets.

If you're planning only one or two small projects, turn directly to the applicable sections for step-by-step instructions.

## Steps in Remodeling

This chart will help you plan the sequence of tasks involved in dismantling your old bathroom and installing the new one. Depending on the size of your job and the materials you select, you may need to alter the suggested order somewhat. Manufacturers' instructions offer additional guidelines.

### Removal sequence
1. Accessories, decorative elements
2. Furniture, if any
3. Contents of cabinets, closets, shelves
4. Fixtures
5. Vanity countertops
6. Vanity cabinets, recessed cabinets, shelves
7. Flooring
8. Light fixtures
9. Wall and ceiling coverings

### Installation sequence
1. Structural changes: walls, doors, windows, skylights
2. Rough plumbing changes
3. Electrical wiring
4. Bathtub, shower
5. Wall and ceiling coverings
6. Light fixtures
7. Vanity cabinet, countertops
8. Toilets, bidets, sinks
9. Wall cabinets, shelves
10. Flooring
11. Decorative elements

Understanding your home's structural shell is a good way to begin any home improvement project, including bathroom remodeling.

Your house's framework probably will conform to the pattern of the typical house shown in the illustration below. Starting at the base of the drawing, you'll notice the following framing members: a wooden sill resting on a foundation wall; a series of horizontal, evenly spaced floor joists; and a subfloor (usually plywood sheets) laid atop the joists. This platform supports the first-floor walls, both interior and exterior. The walls are formed by vertical, evenly spaced studs that run between a horizontal sole plate and parallel top plate. The interior wall coverings are usually fastened directly to the studs.

Depending on the design of the house, one of several types of construction may be used above the first-floor walls. If there's a second story, a layer of ceiling joists rests on the walls; these joists support both the floor above and the ceiling below. A one-story house will have either an "open beamed" ceiling—flat or pitched—or a "finished" ceiling. With a flat roof, the finished ceiling is attached directly to the rafters. The ceiling below a pitched roof is attached to joists.

## REMOVING A PARTITION WALL

Sometimes major bathroom remodeling entails removing all or part of an interior wall to enlarge the space.

Walls that define your bathroom may be bearing or nonbearing. A bearing wall helps support the weight of the house; a nonbearing wall does not. An interior nonbearing wall, often called a partition wall, may be removed without special precautions. The procedure outlined in this section applies only to partitions. If you're considering a remodeling project that involves moving a bearing wall or any wall beneath a second story, consult an architect or contractor about problems and procedures.

How can you tell the difference in walls? All exterior walls running perpendicular to ceiling and floor joists are bearing. At least one main interior wall may be a bearing wall.

To determine whether the wall you're planning to move is bearing, climb up into the attic or crawlspace and check the ceiling joists. If they are joined over any wall, that wall is bearing. Even if joists span the entire width of the house, their midsections may be supported by a bearing wall at the point of maximum allowable span. If you have any doubts about the wall, consult a professional.

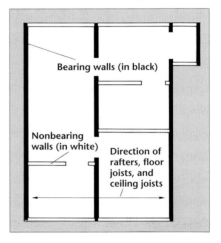

Bearing walls (in black)

Nonbearing walls (in white)

Direction of rafters, floor joists, and ceiling joists

Though removing a partition wall is not complicated, it can be quite messy. Cover the floors and furnishings, and wear a dust mask, safety glasses, and gloves. Ensure adequate ventilation. NOTE: Check the wall for signs of electrical wiring, water and drainpipes, or heating and ventilation ducts; you may have to reroute them.

**Remove the wallcovering.** If there's a door in the wall, remove it from its hinges. Pry off any door trim, ceiling molding, and base molding.

The most common wallcovering is drywall (also called gypsum wallboard) nailed or screwed to wall studs. To remove it, use a pry bar (see "Removing Drywall," page 98).

If the wallcovering is plaster and lath, chisel away the plaster and cut the lath backing—wood strips or metal—so you can pry off large pieces of lath and plaster down to the studs.

## BASIC STRUCTURAL ANATOMY

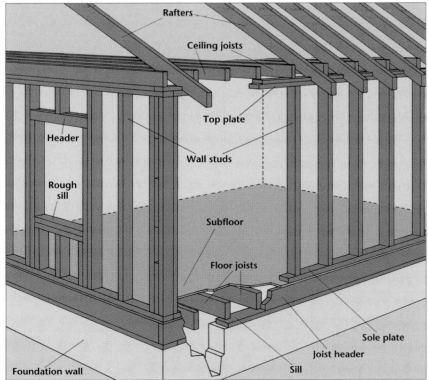

Rafters

Ceiling joists

Top plate

Header

Wall studs

Rough sill

Subfloor

Floor joists

Sole plate

Joist header

Foundation wall

Sill

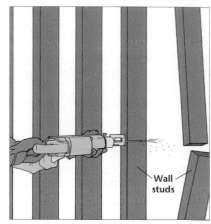

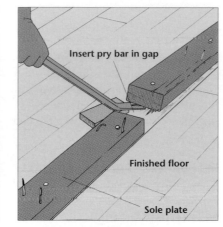

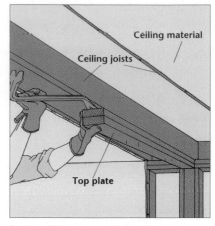

**Saw through the middle** of the wall studs; bend the studs sideways to free the nails from the top and sole plates.

**Cut gaps** through the sole plate with a saw and chisel; insert a pry bar in each side of the gap to free the sole plate.

**Strip ceiling materials** back from the top plate, cut gaps in the plate, and pry out sections of the plate.

**Dismantle the framing.** Remove studs by sawing through the middle of each one; then push and pull them sideways to free the nails (see illustration above).

To remove the sole plate, saw a small section out of the middle down to the finished floor level, chisel through the remaining thickness, and insert a pry bar in the gap.

To remove a top plate that lies parallel to the joists, cut ceiling materials back to adjacent joists and pry off the plate. If the top plate is perpendicular to the joists, you are probably working on a bearing wall and should seek professional advice.

**Patch walls, ceiling, and floor.**
Holes in drywall and plaster aren't difficult to patch; the real challenge lies in matching a special texture, wallpaper, shade of paint, or well-aged floor. This is not a problem if your remodeling plans call for new wallcoverings, ceiling, or flooring. In either case, see the sections "Walls and ceilings" (pages 98–105) and "Flooring" (pages 106–108) for techniques and tips.

## FRAMING A NEW WALL

To subdivide a large bathroom or to enlarge a cramped one, you may need to build a new partition wall or partial wall. Components of wall framing are illustrated at right.

Framing a wall is a straightforward task, but you must measure carefully and check the alignment as work progresses. The basic steps are listed below. To install a doorway, see page 70.

**Plot the location.** The new wall must be anchored securely to existing ceiling joists, the floor, and, at least on one side, to wall studs. To locate the studs, try knocking with your fist along the wall until the sound changes from hollow to solid.

If you have drywall, you can use an electronic stud finder; often, though, the nails or screws that hold drywall to the studs are visible when you look closely at the wall.

To locate ceiling joists, use the same methods or, from the attic or crawlspace, drive small nails down through the ceiling on both sides of a joist to serve as reference points below. Adjacent joists and studs should be evenly spaced, usually about 16 or 24 inches apart.

## WALL FRAMING COMPONENTS

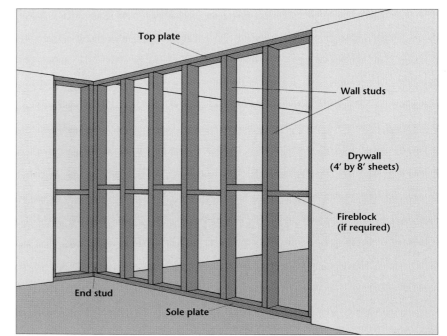

A wall running perpendicular to the joists will demand the least effort to attach. If wall and joists will run parallel, though, try to center the wall under a single joist; otherwise, you'll need to remove ceiling materials between two parallel joists and install nailing blocks every 2 feet between two parallel joists (see illustration at right). If the side of the new wall falls between existing studs, you'll need to install additional nailing blocks.

On the ceiling, mark both ends of the center line of the new wall. Measure 1¾ inches (half the width of the top plate) on both sides of each mark. Snap parallel lines between corresponding marks with a chalk line; the top plate will occupy the space between the lines.

**Position the sole plate.** Hang a plumb bob from each end of the lines you just marked and mark these new points on the floor. Snap two more chalk lines to connect the floor points.

Cut both sole plate and top plate to the desired length. Lay the sole plate between the lines on the floor and nail it in place with 10-penny nails spaced every 2 feet. (If you have a masonry floor, use a masonry bit to drill a bolt hole through the sole plate every 2 or 3 feet. You can then insert expansion anchors for lag bolts and bolt the sole plate to the floor.)

If you're planning a doorway (see "Framing a doorway," at right), don't nail through that section of the plate; it will be cut out later.

**Mark stud positions.** Lay the top plate against the sole plate, as shown in the

## ANCHORING A TOP PLATE

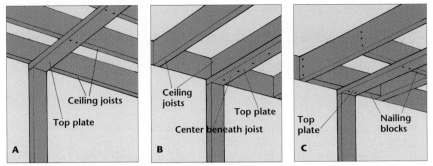

To anchor a top plate, nail to perpendicular joists (A), to the bottom of the parallel joist (B), or install nailing blocks between the parallel joists (C).

illustration below. Beginning at the end that will be attached to an existing stud or to nailing blocks, measure in 1½ inches—the thickness of a 2 by 4 stud—and draw a line across both plates with a combination square. Starting once more from that end, measure and draw lines at 15¼ and 16¾ inches. From these lines, advance 16 inches "on center" (O. C.). Don't worry if the spacing at the far end is less than 16 inches. (If local codes permit, you can consider 24-inch spacing—which will save you lumber— and then adjust the initial placement of lines to 23¼ and 24¾ inches.)

**Fasten the top plate.** While two helpers hold the top plate in position between the lines (marked on the ceiling), nail it to perpendicular joists, to one parallel joist, or to nailing blocks, as shown above.

**Attach the studs.** Measure and cut the studs to exact length. Attach one end stud (or both) to existing studs or

to nailing blocks between studs. Lift the remaining studs into place one at a time; line them up on the marks, and check for plumb using a carpenter's level. Toenail the studs to both the top plate and the sole plate with 8-penny nails.

Some building codes require horizontal fireblocks between studs. The number of rows depends on the code; if permitted, position the blocks to provide an extra nailing surface for wall materials.

**Finish.** After the studs are installed, it's time to add any electrical outlets and switches (see pages 76–80), as well as any new plumbing (see pages 72–75). It's also time for the building inspector to check your work. Following the inspection, you can finish the walls (see pages 98–105).

## FRAMING A DOORWAY

Your remodeling may call for changing the position of a door and creating a new door opening. Be sure the wall you plan to cut into is a nonbearing wall (see page 67). If it's a bearing wall, consult a professional before proceeding.

**Position the opening.** This section assumes that you're installing a standard prehung door and frame. Before starting work, check the manufacturer's "rough opening" dimensions—the exact wall opening required after the new framing is in place.

You'll need to plan an opening large enough to accommodate both

## MARKING STUD POSITIONS

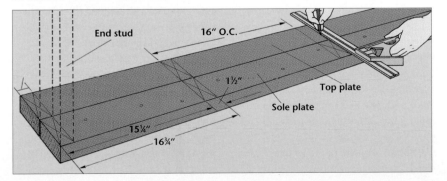

End stud    16" O.C.    1½"    Top plate    Sole plate    15¼"    16¾"

## FRAMING A DOORWAY

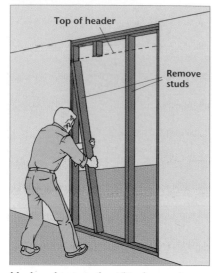

**Mark and cut studs** within the opening, even with the top of the new header.

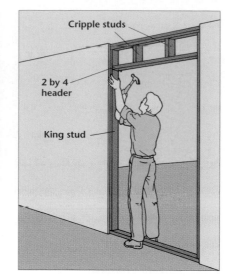

**Nail the new header** to the king studs; nail into ends of the new cripple studs.

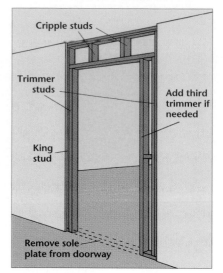

**Nail trimmer studs** to the king studs; block out a third trimmer if needed.

the rough opening and the rough door framing—an additional 1½ inches on top and sides. If your door did not come with rough opening dimensions, add an additional ⅜ inch all around the opening to allow for shimming (adjusting level and plumb) the typical door frame.

Often it's simpler to remove the drywall from floor to ceiling between two bordering studs (the new king studs) that will remain in place. (This is the method illustrated above.) In any case, you'll save work later if you can use at least one existing stud as part of the rough framing.

Regardless of the method you choose, use a carpenter's level for a straightedge, and mark the outline of the opening on the wall.

**Remove wallcovering and studs.** First remove any base molding. Cut along the outline of the opening with a circular saw set to the depth of the wallcovering only, being careful to cut only the drywall, not the studs beneath. Pry the drywall away from the framing. To remove plaster and lath, chisel through plaster to expose lath; then cut the lath and pry it loose.

Cut the studs inside the opening to the height required for the header (see drawing above). Using a combination square, mark these studs on

the face and on one side, then cut carefully with a reciprocating or crosscut saw. Remove the cut studs from the sole plate.

**Frame the opening.** With the wallcovering and studs removed, you're ready to frame the opening. Measure and cut the header (for a partition wall you can use a 2 by 4 laid flat), and toenail it to the king studs with 8-penny nails. Nail the header to the bottoms of the cripple studs.

Cut the part of the sole plate within the opening and pry it away from the subfloor (see "Removing a partition wall," page 67).

Cut trimmer studs and nail them to the king studs with 10-penny nails in a staggered pattern. You'll probably need to adjust the width by blocking out a third trimmer from one side, as shown above right. Remember to leave an extra ⅜ inch on each side for shimming, plus space for the door jambs.

**Hang the door.** A standard prehung door and frame has holes drilled for a lockset. The door comes already fitted and attached to the frame with hinges. Pull out the hinge pins to remove the door before you install the frame. Nail the frame into the rough opening, shimming carefully

to make the side jambs plumb and the head jamb level. Rehang the door and install the lockset; then install stop molding and trim (casing).

## CLOSING A DOORWAY

It's easy to eliminate an existing doorway. Simply add new studs within the opening and attach new wallcoverings. The only trick is to match the present wall surface.

First, remove the casing around the opening. Then remove the door from its hinges or guide track, and pry any jambs or tracks away from the rough framing.

Next, measure the gap on the floor between the existing trimmer studs; cut a length of 2 by 4 to serve as a new sole plate. Nail it to the floor with 10-penny nails. (If you have a masonry floor, attach the 2 by 4 with lag bolts and expansion anchors; see page 69).

Measure and cut new studs to fill the space; position one stud beneath each cripple stud. Toenail the studs to the new sole plate and header with 8-penny nails. Add fireblocks between studs if required by local code.

Strip the wallcoverings back far enough to give yourself a firm nailing surface and an even edge. Then add new coverings to match the existing ones, or resurface the entire wall (see pages 98–105). Match or replace the baseboard molding.

# Adding a skylight

A skylight will bring light and an open feeling into a windowless interior bathroom or to one in which uncovered windows would compromise privacy.

Installing a new skylight in a pitched roof with asphalt or wood shingles is a two-part process: you cut and frame openings in both roof and ceiling, and connect the two openings with a vertical or angled light shaft. (You don't even need a light shaft for a flat roof or an open-beamed ceiling, which requires only a single opening.) A description of the installation sequence follows; for more detailed information, consult the manufacturer's instructions or your skylight dealer.

**Mark the openings.** Begin by measuring and marking the location of the ceiling opening, using the rough opening measurements supplied by the skylight manufacturer. Then drive nails up through the four corners and center so they'll be visible in the attic or crawlspace. You'll save work if you can use one or two ceiling joists as the edges of your opening.

With a plumb bob, transfer the ceiling marks to the underside of the roof. Mark the roof opening suggested by the manufacturer on the underside of the roof and drive nails through the corners.

**Frame the roof opening.** Always exercise extreme caution when working on the roof; if the pitch is steep or if you have a tile or slate roof, you should leave this part to professionals.

If your skylight must be mounted on a curb frame, as in the drawing above, build the curb first; 2 by 6 lumber is commonly used.

To determine the actual size of the opening you need to cut, add the dimensions of any framing materials to the rough opening size marked by the nails. You may need

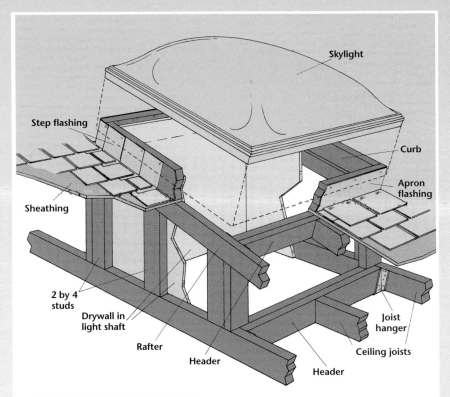

**BASIC PARTS OF A SKYLIGHT**

to remove some extra shingles or roofing materials down to the sheathing to accommodate the flashing of a curb-mounted unit or the flange of a self-flashing unit.

Cut the roof opening in successive layers: roofing materials first; sheathing next, and finally any rafters. Before cutting the rafters, support them with 2 by 4s nailed to the ceiling joists below.

To frame the opening, you'll need double headers and possibly trimmers to narrow the width between rafters.

If you're installing a curb-mounted unit, position and flash the curb. Toenail the curb to the rafters or trimmers and to the headers. Pay special attention to the manufacturer's instructions.

**Mount the skylight.** For a curb-mounted unit, secure the skylight to the top of the curb with nails and a sealant. Nail a self-flashing unit through the flange directly into the

roof sheathing, then coat the joints and nail holes with roofing cement.

**Open the ceiling.** Cut through the ceiling materials and then cut the joists. Support joists to be cut by bracing them against adjacent joists. Frame the opening in the manner used for the roof opening.

**Build a light shaft.** Measure the distance between the ceiling headers and roof headers at each corner and at 16-inch intervals between the corners. Cut studs to fit these measurements and install them as shown in the illustration above. This provides a nailing surface for the wallcovering.

**Make the final touches.** To finish, insulate the spaces between studs in the light shaft. Install drywall by nailing or screwing it to the studs. Painting drywall white maximizes reflected light. Trim the ceiling opening with molding strips.

Whether you're planning to add a single fixture or remodel an entire bathroom, you'll need an introduction to plumbing basics. Replacing an old bathtub, sink, or toilet with a new one at the same location is a straight-forward job, but roughing-in (installing) plumbing for fixtures at new locations takes skill and planning.

What follows is an overview of fundamentals—household plumbing systems, plumbing codes, and general procedures for planning, routing, and roughing-in new pipes. This information may help you to decide whether to make your project a do-it-yourself effort or a professional one. If you have doubts, consider a compromise—you might hire a professional to check your plans and install pipes, then make the fixture hookups yourself (see pages 82–97).

If you want to do all the work yourself, read the information that follows before you begin, to ensure that you're familiar with the tools and techniques required for the job.

## HOW THE SYSTEM WORKS

Three complementary sets of pipes work together to fill your home's plumbing needs: the water supply system, the drain-waste, and the vent (DWV) systems (see the illustration below).

**The supply system.** Water for your toilet, tub, shower, and sink enters the house from a public water main or a source on the property. Water from a water company is usually delivered through a water meter and a main shut-off valve. You'll find the meter either in your basement or crawlspace, or out-doors, near your property line. The main shutoff valve—which turns the water for the whole house on and off—is usually situated near the water meter.

At the water service entrance, the main supply line divides in two—one line branching off to be heated by the water heater, the other remaining as cold water. The two pipes usually run parallel below the first-floor level until they reach the vicinity of a group of fixtures,

then head up through the wall or floor. Sometimes the water supply—hot, cold, or both—passes through a water soften-er or filter before reaching the fixtures.

Supply pipes are installed with a slight pitch in the runs, sloping back toward the lowest point in the system so that all pipes can be drained. Some-times at the lowest point there's a valve that can be opened to drain the sys-tem—essential for vacation homes in cold climates.

### Drain-waste and vent systems.

The drain-waste pipes take advantage of gravity to channel wastewater and solid wastes to the house sewer line. Vent pipes carry away sewer gas and maintain atmospheric pressure in drainpipes and fixture traps. The traps (curved sections in the fixtures' drain-pipes) remain filled with water at all times to keep gases from coming up the drains.

Every house has a 3- or 4-inch-diameter main soil stack that serves a dual function. Below the level of the fixtures it is your home's primary drainpipe; above the stack it becomes a vent with its upper end protruding through the roof. Drainpipes from individual fixtures, as well as branch drains, connect to the main stack. These pipes lead away from all fixtures at a carefully calculated slope—normal-ly ¼ inch per foot. Since any system may clog now and then, cleanouts usu-ally are placed at the upper end of each horizontal section of drainpipe.

A fixture or fixture group located on a branch drain far from the main stack will have a secondary vent stack of its own rising to the roof.

## PLANNING AND LAYOUT

This section outlines the planning process and explores some of your op-tions in adding new plumbing. When plotting out any plumbing addition you must balance code restrictions, the limitations of your system's layout, design considerations, and, of course, your own plumbing abilities.

**A PLUMBING OVERVIEW**

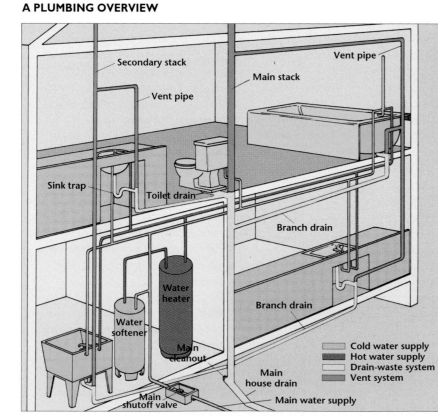

Secondary stack

Vent pipe

Vent pipe

Main stack

Sink trap

Toilet drain

Branch drain

Water heater

Branch drain

Water softener

Main cleanout

Main house drain

Main shutoff valve

Main water supply

Cold water supply
Hot water supply
Drain-waste system
Vent system

**Check the codes.** Almost any improvement that adds pipe to the system will require approval from local building department officials before you start and inspection of the work before you close the walls and floor.

Always learn what work you may do yourself—some codes require that certain work be done only by licensed plumbers.

**Map your system.** A detailed map of your present system will give you a clear picture of where it's feasible to tie into supply and drain lines, and whether the present drains and vents are adequate for the use you plan in the renovation.

Starting in the basement, sketch in the main soil stack, branch drains, house drain, and accessible cleanouts; then trace the networks of hot and cold supply pipes. Also, check the attic or roof for the course of the main stack and any secondary vent stacks. Determine and mark on the sketch the materials and, if possible, the diameters of all pipes (see "Materials," at right).

**Layout options.** Plan the plumbing for any new fixtures in three parts: supply, drainage, and venting. To minimize cost and keep the work simple, arrange a fixture or group of fixtures so they are as close to the present pipes as possible.

Three economical ways to group your new fixtures (see drawings below) are to:

- connect an individual fixture to the existing stack (drawing A)

- add a fixture or group above or below an existing group on the stack

- tie a fixture (except a toilet) directly into a new or existing branch drain (drawing B)

If your addition is planned for an area across the house from the existing plumbing, you'll probably need to run a new secondary vent stack up through the roof, and a new branch drain to the soil stack (see drawing B below) or to the main house drain via an existing cleanout.

The new vent stack must be installed inside an existing wall (a big job), built into a new oversize or "thickened" wall (see "Build a wet wall," page 74), or concealed in a closet or cabinet. In mild climates, a vent may also run up the exterior of the house, but it must be hidden within a box.

**Materials.** Decide what kind of pipe you'll need, based on the material of the pipe you'll be tying into.

Your home's supply pipes most likely are either galvanized steel (referred to as "galvanized" or "iron"

pipe) connected by threaded fittings or are rigid copper joined with soldered fittings.

Older DWV pipes probably are made of cast iron, with "hub" or "bell and spigot" ends joined by molten lead and oakum. (DWV pipes other than the main stack may be galvanized.)

To extend cast-iron pipes, you may substitute "hubless" or no-hub fittings (made of neoprene gaskets and stainless steel clamps), which are simpler to install than hubbed fittings.

If you wish to change pipe material in your extension, it's a matter of inserting the appropriate adapter at the fitting end. You might want to change cast-iron or galvanized pipe to copper or plastic pipe. First check your local code, because some areas prohibit use of plastic pipe.

## PLUMBING CODES

Few code restrictions apply to simple extensions of hot and cold water supply pipes, provided your house's water pressure is up to the task. The material and diameter for supply pipes serving each new fixture or appliance are spelled out clearly in the plumbing code. More troublesome are the pipes that make up the DWV system. Codes are quite specific about the following: the size of stacks, drainpipes, and vents serving any new fixture requiring drainage; the critical distance from fixture traps to the stack; and the method of venting fixtures.

**Stack, vent, and drain sizes.** The plumbing code will specify minimum diameters for stacks and vents in relation to numbers of fixture units. (One fixture unit represents 7.5 gallons or 1 cubic foot of water per minute.) In the code you'll find fixture unit ratings for all plumbing fixtures given in chart form.

To determine drainpipe diameter, look up the fixture or fixtures you're considering on the code's fixture unit chart. Add up the total fixture units; then look up the drain diameter specified for that number of units.

## PLUMBING LAYOUT OPTIONS

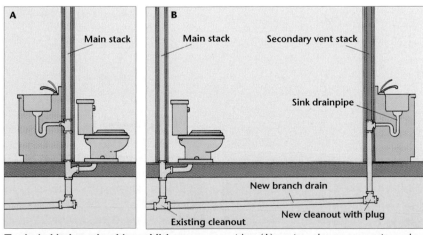

**To drain kitchen plumbing additions,** you can either (A) tap into the present main stack, if nearby, or (B) install a new branch drain and secondary vent stack.

Vent pipe sizing criteria also include the length of vent and type of vent, in addition to fixture unit load.

**Critical distance.** The maximum distance allowed between a fixture's trap and the stack or main drain that it empties into is called the critical distance. No drain outlet may be completely below the level of the trap's crown weir (see illustration below)—if it were, it would act as a siphon, draining the trap. Thus, when the ideal drainpipe slope of ¼ inch per foot is figured in, the length of that drainpipe quickly becomes limited. But if the fixture drain is vented properly within the critical distance, the drainpipe may run on indefinitely to the actual stack or main drain.

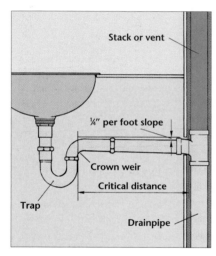

**Venting options.** The four basic venting options (see illustration above right)—subject to local code—are wet venting, back venting, individual venting, and indirect venting.

- Wet venting is simplest—the fixture is vented directly through the fixture drain to the soil stack.

- Back venting (reventing) involves running a vent loop up past the fixture to reconnect with the main stack or secondary vent above the fixture level.

- Individual (secondary) venting means running a secondary vent stack up through the roof for a

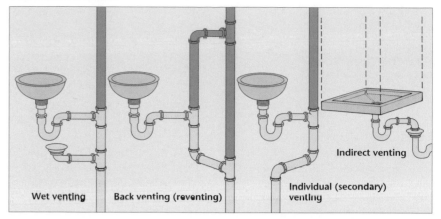

Wet venting    Back venting (reventing)    Individual (secondary) venting    Indirect venting

new fixture or group of fixtures distant from the main stack.

- Indirect venting allows you to vent some fixtures (such as a basement shower) into a laundry tub or into an existing floor drain without the need for further venting.

## ROUGHING-IN NEW PLUMBING

Once you've planned your plumbing additions, you can begin installation.

**Locate and tie into existing pipe.** In the mapping stage, you determined the rough locations of the pipes. The next step is to pinpoint them and cut away wall, ceiling, or floor coverings along studs or joists to expose the sections you want to tie in to. Be sure to cut out holes large enough to allow you to work comfortably. (For information about wall and floor coverings, see pages 98–108.)

Basically, tying into drain-waste, vent, and supply lines entails cutting a section out of each pipe and inserting a new fitting to join old and new pipe. The method you use to tie into the pipes varies with the pipe material.

**Route new pipes.** With the connections made, the new DWV and supply pipes are run to the new fixture location. Ideally, new drainpipes should be routed below the bathroom floor. They can be suspended from the floor joists by pipe hangers, inserted in the space between parallel joists, or run through notches or holes drilled in

joists that are at right angles to the pipe (if allowed by code). If you have a finished basement or your bathroom is on the second floor, you'll need to cut into the floor or ceiling to install pipes between or through joists, hide the pipes with a dropped ceiling, or box them in. (Remember that drainpipes must slope away from fixtures at a minimum slope of ¼ inch per foot.)

Supply pipes normally follow drainpipes but can be routed directly up through the wall or floor from main horizontal lines. Supply pipes should run parallel, at least 6 inches apart. In cold areas, codes may prohibit supply pipes in exterior walls.

**Build a wet wall.** The main soil stack, and often a secondary stack, commonly hide inside an oversize house wall called a "wet wall."

Unlike an ordinary 2 by 4 stud wall (shown on page 68), a wet wall has a sole plate and a top plate built from 2 by 6 or 2 by 8 lumber. Additionally, the 2 by 4 studs are set in pairs, with flat sides facing out. This creates maximum space inside the wall for large DWV pipes (which often have an outer diameter greater than 3½ inches) and for fittings, which are wider yet.

You can also "fur out" an existing wall to hide added pipes: attach new 2 by 4s to the old ones, and add new wallcoverings. Similarly, a new branch drain that cannot run below the floor may be hidden by a raised section of floor.

## ROUGHING-IN FIXTURES

Following are general notes on roughing-in new fixtures that require tying into your present DWV and supply systems, or extending them. Note that fixtures may be required to have air chambers—dead-end pipes that minimize noisy water hammer.

**Sink.** A sink is comparatively easy to install. Common installations are back to back (requires little pipe), within a vanity cabinet (hides pipe runs), and side by side. A sink can often be wet vented if it's within the critical distance; otherwise it's back vented. Adding a sink has little impact on the drain's present efficiency (a sink rates low in fixture units).

The supply pipes needed include hot and cold stubouts with shutoff valves; transition fittings, if necessary; and flexible tubing above shutoff valves (see "Sink faucets," page 92).

**Toilet.** The single most troublesome fixture to install, a toilet requires its own vent (2-inch minimum) and at least a 3-inch drain. If it's on a branch drain, a toilet can't be upstream from a sink or shower.

The closet bend and toilet floor flange must be roughed-in first; the floor flange must be positioned to be at the level of the eventual finished floor.

The supply pipes needed include a cold water stubout with shutoff valve and flexible tubing above the valve (see "Installing a toilet," page 95).

**Shower stall and bathtub.** Like sinks, bathtubs and showers rate low in fixture units. They're often positioned on branch drains and are usually wet vented or back vented; both enter the stack at floor level or below because of the below-floor trap. A shower's faucet body and shower head assembly are installed while the wall is open; tubs and showers may require support framing.

The supply pipes needed include hot and cold supply lines and a pipe to the shower head (see "Tub and shower faucets," pages 93–94).

## ROUGHING-IN FIXTURES

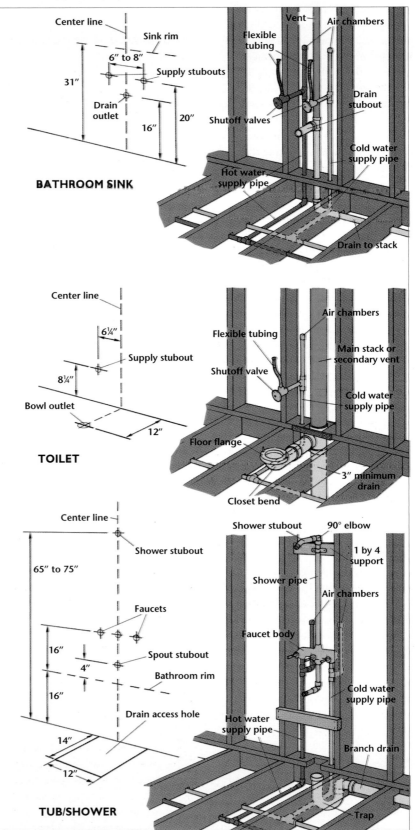

**Representative roughing-in measurements.** Plumbing components illustrated above are a sink, toilet, and tub/shower. Use these measurements to help you plan; check local codes and specific fixture dimensions for exact roughing-in requirements.

What may appear to be a hopelessly tangled maze of wires running through the walls, under the floors, and above the ceiling of your home is actually a well-organized system composed of several electrical circuits. In your bathroom, those circuits supply power to the light fixtures, switches, fans, heaters, and electrical outlets.

This section briefly explains your home's electrical system and offers general information about basic electrical improvements so you can better understand the processes involved in making changes to your electrical system. Techniques for installing light fixtures appear on pages 79–80.

Before you do any work yourself, talk with your building department's electrical inspector about local codes, the National Electrical Code (NEC), and your area's requirements for permits and inspections.

## UNDERSTANDING YOUR SYSTEM

Today most homes have what's called "three wire" service. The utility company connects three wires to your service entrance panel. Each of two hot wires supplies electricity at approximately 120 volts. A third wire—a neutral one—is maintained at zero volts. (Don't be misled, though; all three wires are live.)

Three-wire service provides both 120-volt and 240-volt capabilities. One hot wire and the neutral wire combine to provide 120 volts—primarily for lights and plug-in outlets. Two hot wires combine to produce 240 volts, often used for electric heaters.

**Service entrance panel.** This panel is the control center for your electrical system. Inside the panel you'll usually find the main disconnect (main fuses or circuit breaker), the fuses or circuit breakers protecting each individual circuit, and the grounding connection for the entire system.

## ROUTING CABLE TO OUTLETS

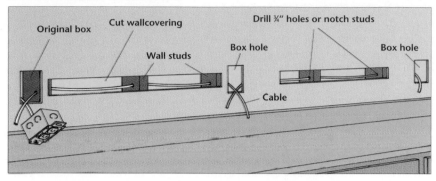

Original box · Cut wallcovering · Wall studs · Drill ¾" holes or notch studs · Box hole · Box hole · Cable

**Simple circuitry.** The word "circuit" means the course electric current travels—in a continuous path from the service entrance panel or a separate subpanel, through one or more devices in your home that use electricity (such as light fixtures or appliances), and back to the panel. The devices are connected to the circuit by parallel wiring. With parallel wiring, a hot, a neutral, and a ground wire (for a 120-volt circuit) run unbroken from one fixture box, outlet box, or switch box to another. Wires branch off to individual electrical devices from these continuous wires.

Modern circuit wires are housed together in a cable. Cable contains either one or two hot wires, a neutral

### An exception to the color-code rule

We often assume that a white wire is always a neutral wire. Wires that are black or red are always hot. In some cases, a white wire may substitute as a hot (black) wire. For example, a switch loop can be wired with a two-wire cable that is purchased with one black wire and one white wire, in which case the white wire substitutes as the current-carrying wire going from the source to the switch. A good safety practice is to paint the hot white wire black at the ends.

wire, and a ground wire—each, except the ground wire, wrapped in its own insulation. (For the best connections, use only cable with all-copper wire.)

Individual wires are color coded for easy identification. Hot wires are usually black or red. Neutral wires are white or gray. And grounding wires are bare copper or green.

Occasionally, a white wire will be used as a hot wire; if so, it should be taped or painted black near terminals and splices for easy identification.

**Grounding.** The NEC requires that every circuit have a ground wire. This provides an auxiliary path to ground for any short that might occur in a fixture or appliance. Also, according to the NEC, all outlets in a bathroom, regardless of their proximity to a water source, must be protected with ground-fault circuit interrupters (GFCIs). These cut off power within $\frac{1}{40}$ of a second if current begins leaking anywhere along the circuit. They may be special circuit breakers or built into an outlet.

## EXTENDING A CIRCUIT

To extend an existing electrical circuit, you'll need a knack for making wire connections, and the patience to route new cable.

Before you start work, remember: NEVER WORK ON ANY LIVE CIRCUIT, FIXTURE, PLUG-IN OUTLET, OR SWITCH. Your life may depend on it. Turn off the circuit breaker or remove the fuse, and make sure no one but you can turn the electricity back on.

The steps in extending a circuit are outlined below. Generally, you route new cable from box to box; you install new boxes where you want to add outlets, fixtures, or switches; and then you tap into a power source—an existing outlet, switch, or fixture box.

To install a new circuit, the work is much the same, except that you connect into a service panel or subpanel instead of into an existing outlet, switch, or fixture box.

### Select a power source.
A circuit can be tapped for power at almost any accessible outlet, switch, or fixture box of the appropriate voltage. (The exceptions are a switch box without a neutral wire and a fixture box at the end of a circuit.) The box you tap into must be large enough to hold new wires in addition to existing wires and must have knockout holes through which you can run the new cable.

### Select and locate new boxes.
If wall or ceiling coverings have not yet been installed, choose an outlet or switch box you nail to studs or joists. If wall or ceiling coverings are already in place, those cut-in boxes don't have to be secured to studs or joists. Requirements regarding boxes for mounting ceiling fixtures are outlined on pages 79–80.

Unless codes prohibit the use of plastic, you can use either plastic or metal boxes. Metal boxes, though sturdier, must be grounded; plastic boxes cost less and need not be grounded, though the circuit must have a ground wire.

To find a suitable box location, turn off power to all circuits that may be behind the wall or ceiling. Drill a small test hole and probe through it with a length of stiff insulated wire until you find an empty space.

Unless old boxes are at different levels, place new outlet boxes 12 to 18 inches above the floor, switch boxes or outlet boxes above a counter 44 inches above the floor. Never place boxes near a tub,

shower, or tub/shower unit.

If you're adding a new wall, you may be required by code to add an outlet every 12 feet, or one per wall regardless of the wall's length.

When you've determined the correct locations, trace the outline of each box on the wall or ceiling (omit the protruding brackets). Then cut carefully along the outlines and remove the wallcovering.

### Route and connect new cable.
After the box holes are cut, run cable from the power source to each new box location. (Wait until you have the new boxes wired and the outlets, switches, and fixtures connected before you make the actual hookup to the source.)

Where you have access from an unfinished basement, an unfloored attic, or a garage adjacent to the bathroom, it's easy to run cable either parallel to and attached to the joists or studs or perpendicular through holes drilled in them.

Where walls and ceilings are covered on both sides, you'll have to fish cable through them, using electrician's fish tape (illustrated below) or a length of stiff wire with one end bent into a blunt, tight hook. Two wires may be required to work around corners.

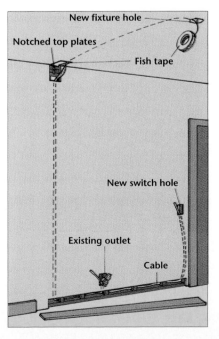

New fixture hole
Notched top plates
Fish tape
New switch hole
Existing outlet
Cable

After routing the new cable, secure the cable to each new box. Slip a cable connector onto the end of the cable and insert the cable and the connector into a knockout in the box. Fasten the connector to the box, leaving about 6 to 8 inches of cable sticking out for the wiring connections. Then mount the box to the ceiling or wall and wire as described below.

### Wire plug-in outlets.
An outlet must have the same amperage and voltage rating as the circuit. If you have aluminum wiring, be sure to use the correct outlet; it will be identified by the letters CO-ALR. An outlet marked CU-AL should be used only with copper wire. If you are installing a GFCI outlet, follow the manufacturer's directions.

The illustration below shows how to wire a plug-in bathroom outlet with both halves live. The box is assumed to be metal; if you use a plastic box, there's no need to ground the box, but you'll have to attach a grounding wire to each outlet. To do this, simply loop the end of the wire under the grounding screw. Then you can connect the hot wire to the brass screw of the outlet, the neutral wire to the silver screw, and the ground wire to the green screw.

### WIRING PLUG-IN OUTLETS

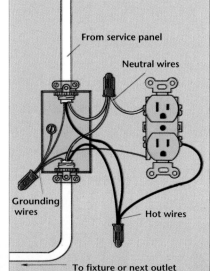

From service panel
Neutral wires
Grounding wires
Hot wires
To fixture or next outlet

## WIRING SINGLE-POLE SWITCHES

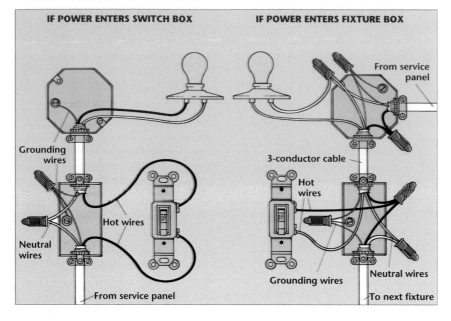

**IF POWER ENTERS SWITCH BOX**

Grounding wires

Hot wires

Neutral wires

From service panel

**IF POWER ENTERS FIXTURE BOX**

From service panel

3-conductor cable

Hot wires

Grounding wires

Neutral wires

To next fixture

## WIRING A GFCI

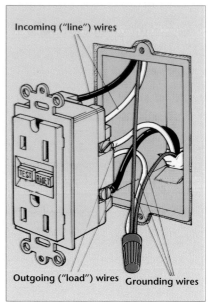

Incoming ("line") wires

Outgoing ("load") wires

Grounding wires

**Wire single-pole switches.** One single-pole switch may control one or more light fixtures, a heater, a ventilating fan, or several outlets.

Just like outlets, the switch must have the same amperage and voltage rating as the circuit. If you have aluminum wiring, be sure to use a switch that is marked with the letters CO-ALR.

When wiring switches, remember that they are installed only on hot wires. Because the toggles on most

home switches like those illustrated above are made of shockproof plastic, these switches do not need to be grounded. If switches are housed in plastic boxes, the boxes do not need to be grounded. However, grounding wires always provide an extra safety precaution. When installing a plastic switch box at the end of a circuit, secure the end of the grounding wire between the switch bracket and the mounting screw. If the switch is in the middle of a circuit, just twist the

ends of the ground wires together and cover them with a wirenut.

Single-pole switches have two screw terminals of the same color (usually brass) for wire connections, and a definite right-side up. You should be able to read the words ON and OFF embossed on the toggle. It doesn't make any difference which hot wire goes to which terminal. The cable can be run either first to the fixture or first to the switch—whichever route is the more convenient one.

## WIRING INTO A POWER SOURCE

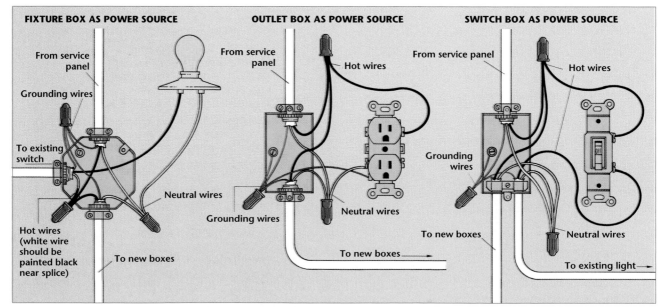

**FIXTURE BOX AS POWER SOURCE**

From service panel

Grounding wires

To existing switch

Hot wires (white wire should be painted black near splice)

To new boxes

**OUTLET BOX AS POWER SOURCE**

From service panel

Hot wires

Grounding wires

Neutral wires

To new boxes

**SWITCH BOX AS POWER SOURCE**

From service panel

Hot wires

Grounding wires

To new boxes

Neutral wires

To existing light

**Wire a GFCI.** The protection value of an outlet-style ground-fault circuit interrupter (GFCI) has made it standard in new construction. Depending on the model, the GFCI may also protect all other devices downstream (away from the source) from it, but it will not protect any outlets upstream (toward the source).

A GFCI receptacle is wired like an ordinary outlet, except that you must connect incoming hot and neutral wires to the "line," or input, terminals, and any outgoing wires to the "load" side. If your model includes a built-in grounding jumper, attach it to the other ground wires in the box with a wirenut, as shown in the illustration on page 78, top right.

**Wire into the power source.** After you have wired new outlets and new switches, you are ready to make the final connections. Connections to three types of boxes used as power sources are shown in the drawings on the bottom of page 78. Wirenuts join

and protect the stripped ends of the spliced wires within the boxes.

## INSTALLING LIGHT FIXTURES

Most bathrooms need both task lighting for specific areas and general lighting. For a discussion of lighting choices, see pages 48–49.

Basically, to replace an existing light fixture with one of the same type, you disconnect the wires to the old fixture and connect them to the new fixture. Adding a new fixture where there was none before is more complicated. You must first run new cable from a power source and install a fixture box and a switch.

Below are instructions for installing two types of light fixtures—surface mounted and recessed.

**Surface-mounted fixtures.** You can attach these fixtures directly to a wall or ceiling fixture box, or suspend ceiling fixtures from a fixture box by chains or cord. New fixtures usually come with their own mounting hard-

ware, adaptable to any fixture box.

Sometimes the weight of the new fixture or the wiring needed for proper grounding requires you to replace the box before you install the fixture.

Electrical code requirements sometimes allow ceiling fixtures weighing less than 24 ounces to be mounted on cut-in boxes held in position by the ceiling material. For a more secure installation and for all heavier fixtures, you must fasten the box to a framing member or a special bracket secured to the joists. Do not attach fixtures heavier than 6 pounds to the box with screws through the fixture's metal canopy; use the hardware supplied by the manufacturer or check with an electrician or your local electrical inspector.

A cord or chain-hung fixture must have a grounding wire run from the socket to the box. Most new fixtures are prewired with a grounding wire.

Then install your new surface-mounted fixture as described and illustrated on page 80.

## SURFACE-MOUNTED FIXTURES

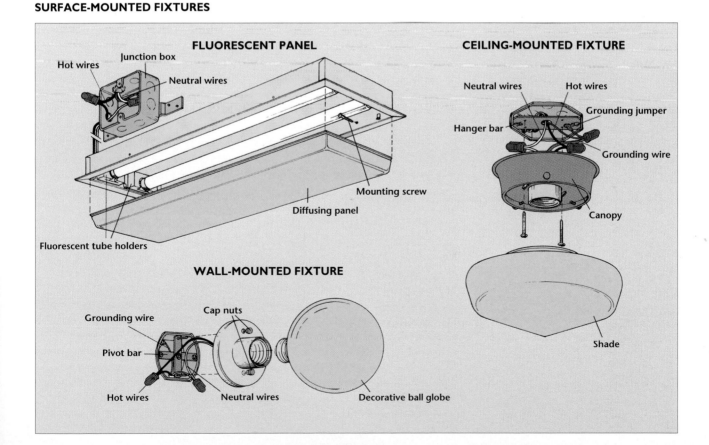

**FLUORESCENT PANEL**
Hot wires
Junction box
Neutral wires
Mounting screw
Diffusing panel
Fluorescent tube holders

**CEILING-MOUNTED FIXTURE**
Neutral wires
Hot wires
Grounding jumper
Hanger bar
Grounding wire
Canopy
Shade

**WALL-MOUNTED FIXTURE**
Grounding wire
Cap nuts
Pivot bar
Hot wires
Neutral wires
Decorative ball globe

- To replace an existing fixture with a new one, first turn off the circuit. Remove the shade, if any, from the old fixture. Unscrew the canopy from the fixture box, and detach the mounting bar if there is one. Now make a sketch of how the wires are connected. If the wires are spliced with wirenuts, unscrew them and untwist the wires. If the wires are spliced and wrapped with electrician's tape, simply unwind the tape and untwist the wires. Match the wires of the new fixture to the old wires shown in your sketch, and splice with wirenuts. Secure the new fixtures as recommended by the manufacturer, using any new hardware included.

- To install a fixture in a new location, you must route a new cable from a power source and install new fixture and switch boxes. New cable routed to the fixture box should include a grounding wire to be attached to the box's grounding screw. If more than one cable enters the box (for example, a separate cable from the switch box), you'll need to attach the end of a short length of bare 12-gauge wire (a "jumper") to the grounding

### RECESSED DOWNLIGHTS

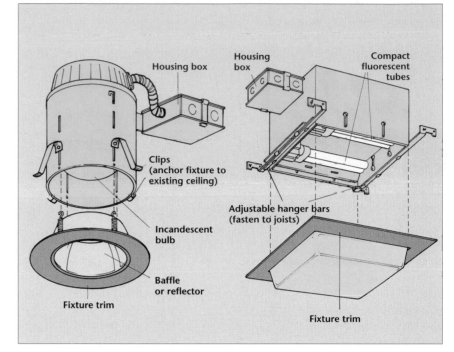

Housing box

Clips (anchor fixture to existing ceiling)

Incandescent bulb

Baffle or reflector

Fixture trim

Housing box

Compact fluorescent tubes

Adjustable hanger bars (fasten to joists)

Fixture trim

### ONE CABLE

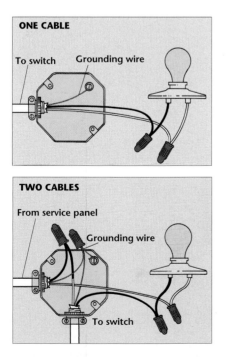

To switch — Grounding wire

### TWO CABLES

From service panel

Grounding wire

To switch

screw, and use a wirenut to splice the other end to the ends of the grounding wires in the cables.

Once you've routed the new cable and grounded the fixture box, wire in the new fixture—black wire to black, white to white; cap all splices with wirenuts. Then mount the fixture with hardware supplied by the manufacturer.

**Recessed ceiling fixtures.** Common recessed fixtures include incandescent circular or square downlights and larger fluorescent ceiling, or "troffer," panels. You'll need to cut a hole in the ceiling between the joists, or remove tiles or panels from a suspended ceiling, to install either type. Larger troffer panels may also require 2 by 4 blocking between joists for support.

Recessed fixtures need several inches of clearance above the finished ceiling. They're most easily installed below an unfinished attic or crawlspace. Because of the heat generated by many downlights, you must either buy a special zero-clearance model (type ICT) or plan to remove insulation within 3 inches of the fixture and make sure that no other combustible materials come within ½ inch.

Most low-voltage downlights come

with an integral transformer attached to the frame; if yours doesn't, you'll first need to mount an external transformer nearby and then route wire to the fixture.

If there's no crawlspace above the ceiling, find the joists (see pages 67–68). Don't forget to shut off power to any circuits that might be wired behind the ceiling before drilling exploratory holes (or doing any work).

Once you've determined the proper location for the fixture housing, trace its outline on the ceiling with a pencil; use a keyhole saw or saber saw to cut the hole. Brace a plaster ceiling as you cut.

If you don't have access from above, shop for a remodeling fixture. The version shown above, at left, slips through the ceiling hole and clips onto the edge of the ceiling. The fixture trim then snaps onto the housing from below. (Remember to hook up the wires to the circuit before securing the fixture and trim.)

So-called new work or rough-in downlights with adjustable hanger bars, such as the model shown above at right, are easy to install from above. Simply nail the ends of the bars to joists on either side; then clip the trim or baffle into place from below.

# Climate control

Certain elements of your bathroom's climate—steam, excess heat, early morning chill—can be annoying and unpleasant. When you remodel your bathroom, consider adding an exhaust fan to freshen the air and draw out destructive moisture, and a heater to warm you on cool days. Installing these climate controllers is within the grasp of most do-it-yourselfers. For more details on both fans and heaters, see page 61.

## HEATING THE BATHROOM

Because electric heaters are easy to install and clean to operate, they're the most popular choice for heating bathrooms. In addition to the standard wall and ceiling-mounted units, you will find heaters combined with exhaust fans, lights, or both. Many units require a dedicated 120 or 240-volt circuit, so shop carefully.

Gas heaters that can be recessed into a wall between two studs so they are flush with the wall are available in a variety of styles and sizes. Regardless of how they heat, all gas models require a gas supply line and must be vented to the outside.

Choose the location of your heater carefully. Of course, you'll want to place it where someone getting out of the tub or shower will benefit from it (this is particularly true of radiant heaters, which heat objects directly). But don't locate the heater where someone will bump against its hot surfaces, or where it might char or ignite curtains, towels, or a rug or bathmat.

Since gas heaters require a vent to the outside, you'll probably want to place the heater on an outside wall. Otherwise, you'll have to run the vent through the attic or crawlspace and out through the roof. It's best to have a professional run gas lines; in any case, whether you do the work yourself or not, you must have the work tested and inspected before the gas is turned on.

## VENTILATING THE BATHROOM

You can buy fans to mount in the wall or ceiling. Some models are combined with a light or a heater; some have both.

It's important that your exhaust fan have adequate capacity. The Home Ventilating Institute (HVI) recommends that the fan be capable of exchanging the air at least eight times every hour. To determine the required fan capacity in cubic feet per minute (CFM) for a bathroom with an 8-foot ceiling, multiply the room's length and width in feet by 1.1.

For example, if your bathroom is 6 by 9 feet, you would calculate the required fan capacity as follows:

6 x 9 x 1.1 = 59.4 CFM

Rounding off, you would need fan capacity of at least 60 CFM. If your fan must exhaust through a long duct or several elbows, you'll need greater capacity to overcome the increased resistance. Follow the dealer's or manufacturer's recommendations.

Ideally, your fan should be mounted as close to the shower or tub as it can be. It should also be as far away as possible from the source of replacement air (the door, for instance). In addition, you'll want the exhaust duct to be as short and straight as possible. If you have trouble finding a location that meets all three requirements, you may want to consult a professional.

**THREE WAYS TO DUCT EXHAUST FANS**

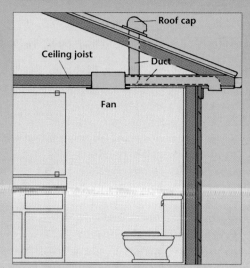

**Ceiling fan** ventilates through duct either to roof cap on roof or to grill in soffit under the eave.

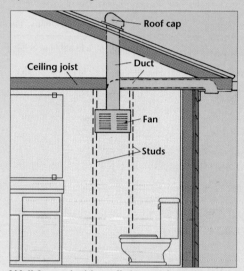

**Wall fan on inside wall** also ventilates through duct to cap on roof or to grill in soffit under eave.

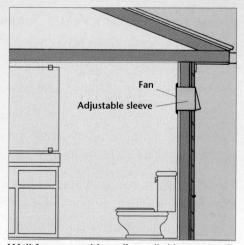

**Wall fan on outside wall,** installed between wall studs, ventilates through wall directly to outside.

Replacing the bathroom sink (also called a lavatory or basin) is one of the quickest ways to give a bathroom a new look without getting involved in a more complex and expensive remodeling project.

This section will show you how to remove and install the four basic types of sinks: an integral sink and countertop, and pedestal, wall-hung, and deck-mount sinks. For further information on the variety of sink models and materials, see page 56.

If you're planning to add a new sink or to move an old one, you may want to consult a professional about extending the supply, drain, and vent lines (see pages 72–75). But to replace a sink, extensive plumbing experience is not a requirement.

## REMOVING A SINK

Unless you're installing a new floor covering, be sure to protect the bathroom floor with a piece of cardboard or plywood before you begin work. You'll also want a bucket and a supply of rags or sponges nearby to soak up excess water.

To loosen corroded plumbing connections, douse them with penetrating oil an hour before you start.

### DISCONNECTING THE PLUMBING

If the sink faucet is mounted on the countertop and you don't plan to replace the faucet, it isn't necessary to disconnect the water supply lines. If the faucet is connected to the sink, you do need to disconnect the supply lines.

Be sure to turn off the water at the sink shutoff valves or at the main valve before doing any work. Disconnect the supply lines at the shutoff valves, placing a bucket underneath them to catch any water, and open the faucets so the lines can drain.

If your sink isn't equipped with shutoff valves, disconnect the supply lines at the faucet inlet shanks, as

explained on pages 92–93, and plan to add shutoff valves before you connect the plumbing to the new sink (or have a professional plumber do the work).

Next, move the bucket underneath the trap. If the trap has a cleanout plug, remove it to drain the water, then loosen the slip nuts and remove the trap. If there is no cleanout plug, remove the trap and dump the water into the bucket.

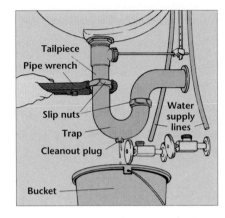

Disconnect the pop-up drain assembly by loosening the clevis screw (see page 93) and then removing the spring clip that connects the stopper and pivot rod to the pop-up rod on the faucet (see "Removing a Sink Faucet," page 92).

The tailpiece, drain body, and sink flange, as well as the faucet, will not come out with the sink. If you plan to reuse the old faucet, remove it carefully from the sink and set it aside.

### REMOVING AN INTEGRAL SINK AND COUNTERTOP

An integral sink is molded as part of the countertop, and the unit is secured to the top of a vanity cabinet. Look underneath for any metal clips or wooden braces that secure the unit to the vanity, and remove them. Then lift off the whole unit.

If you can't remove the unit easily, insert the end of a small pry bar in the joint between the countertop and vanity cabinet at a back corner (see illustration above right). Carefully lift up the pry bar to break the sealing material between the countertop and the vanity. If the joint is too narrow to accept the end of a pry bar, you can cut through the sealing material

with a hot putty knife, then pry or lift up the countertop.

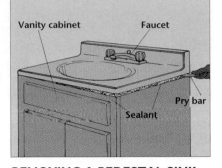

### REMOVING A PEDESTAL SINK

Most pedestal sinks are made of two pieces—the sink and the pedestal or base. Look in the opening at the rear of the pedestal to locate a nut or bolt holding the sink down. If you find one, remove it. Lift off the sink and set it aside. Some older pedestal sinks may also have a metal bracket under the sink that connects it to the wall.

The pedestal is usually bolted to the floor. You may find the bolts on the base or on the inside of the pedestal (see illustration top left, page 83). Undo the bolts and remove the pedestal. If you can't move it after removing the bolts, rock it back and forth, then lift it out. If the pedestal is recessed into a ceramic tile floor, you may have to remove the surrounding floor tiles with a cold chisel and soft-headed steel hammer. Rock the pedestal back and forth to break any remaining seal with the floor. Lift the pedestal up and set it aside.

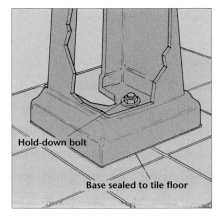

Hold-down bolt

Base sealed to tile floor

## REMOVING A WALL-HUNG SINK

To remove a wall-hung sink, first un-screw the legs, if any, that support the front of the sink. Check underneath for any bolts securing the sink to the mounting bracket on the wall (see the illustration below) and remove them. Then lift the sink straight up and off the mounting bracket.

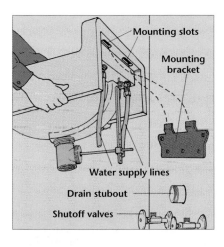

Mounting slots

Mounting bracket

Water supply lines

Drain stubout

Shutoff valves

## REMOVING A DECK-MOUNT SINK

There are three basic types of deck-mount sinks used in vanity counter-tops: self-rimmed sinks, rimmed sinks, and undermounted sinks. All may be secured to the countertop with lugs or clamps that must be unscrewed before you remove the sink.

**Self-rimmed sinks.** These sinks have a molded flange that sits on the counter-top. Once you have removed any lugs or clamps from underneath, use a hot putty knife or other knife to cut through the sealing material between

sink and countertop; then pry up the sink to break the seal and lift it out.

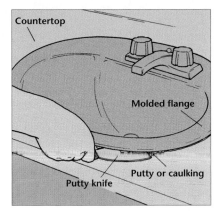

Countertop

Molded flange

Putty or caulking

Putty knife

**Rimmed sinks.** Have a helper support the sink while you undo the lugs or clamps that secure the sink's metal rim to the countertop. (If you're working alone, you can support the sink with a 2 by 4 and a wood block tied together through the drain; see the illustration below.) After you remove the lugs or clamps, cut through the sealing materi-al between the rim and the countertop with a hot putty knife or other knife. Pry up the rim to free the sink, then lift it straight up.

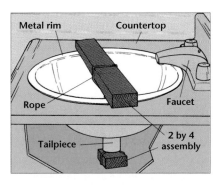

Metal rim        Countertop

Rope

Tailpiece

Faucet

2 by 4 assembly

**Undermounted sinks.** An unrimmed or recessed sink is secured to the under-side of the countertop. The easiest way to remove such a sink is to first take off the countertop. Check below for any brackets and remove them. Then insert a pry bar into the joint between the countertop and the vanity cabinet near a rear corner, and pry up the countertop. Turn it bottom side up and rest it on a padded surface. Undo the lugs or clamps securing the sink, and lift the sink off the countertop.

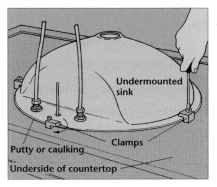

Undermounted sink

Putty or caulking        Clamps

Underside of countertop

With a tiled countertop, the flange usually rests on top of the plywood base for the tile. Look underneath; if you do not see any clips or brackets, you will have to remove the tile surrounding the edge of the sink. With a ball-peen hammer and a cold chisel, carefully remove enough tile so that you can lift the sink from the countertop. (Be sure to protect your eyes with goggles, and wear gloves.) If you can't find matching replacement tile and need to reuse the old tiles, remove them carefully to avoid breaking them.

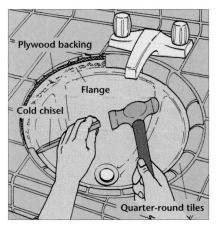

Plywood backing

Flange

Cold chisel

Quarter-round tiles

## INSTALLING A SINK

If you're installing a sink at a new location instead of replacing an existing one, you'll need to extend the supply, drain, and vent pipes (for help, see pages 72–75). If you'd like your sink to be higher than standard, you can raise the vanity of an integral or deck-mount sink by building a base under it. If you're installing a wall-hung sink, simply mount the bracket higher. You can't adjust the height of a pedestal sink, but you may be able to buy a taller model.

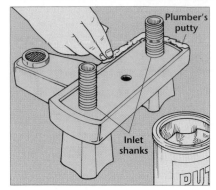

**Apply putty** to bottom edge of the faucet if there is no rubber gasket to seal it to sink's surface.

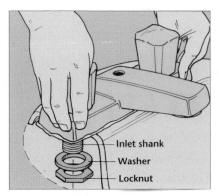

**Set the faucet** in place, insert the inlet shanks through the sink holes, and press down. Add washers and locknuts.

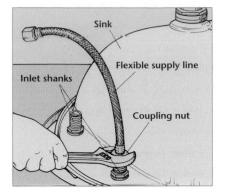

**Attach flexible supply lines** to the faucet's inlet shanks, using pipe joint compound and coupling nuts.

Before installing the sink, you will have to install both the faucet and the sink flange.

## INSTALLING THE FAUCET AND SINK FLANGE

Whether the faucet is to be mounted on the countertop or on the sink itself, you'll find it easier to install the faucet before you set the sink in place. The main steps are illustrated above. First make sure that the mounting surface is clean. If your faucet came with a rubber gasket, place it on the bottom of the faucet. For a faucet without a gasket, put a bead of plumber's putty around the bottom edge of the faucet.

Then gently set the faucet in position and press it down onto the sink or countertop surface. Assemble the washers and locknuts on the inlet shanks, then tighten the nuts. Remove excess putty from around the faucet. Connect the supply lines to the inlet shanks and tighten the coupling nuts. For more detailed information on installing faucets, see pages 92–93.

Now install the sink flange and drain. To attach the flange, run a bead of plumber's putty around the drain hole of the sink. Press the flange into the puttied hole. Put the locknut, metal washer, and flat rubber washer on the drain body in that order. Insert the threaded end of the drain body into the bottom of the sink and screw it onto the flange. Then tighten the locknut until it is snug (but be careful not to overtighten).

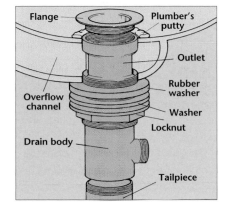

## INSTALLING AN INTEGRAL SINK AND COUNTERTOP

Cover the top edges of the vanity cabinet with a sealant recommended by the manufacturer. Place the countertop unit on the cabinet flush with the back edge. Make sure the overhang—if any—is equal on the left and right sides. Press along the countertop edges to complete the seal, and check around the perimeter, being careful to remove any excess sealant.

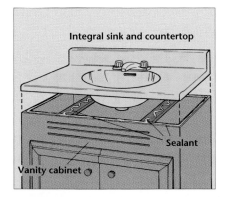

If your unit came with mounting brackets, use them to secure the countertop to the vanity. Seal the joint between the countertop and the wall with caulking compound.

## INSTALLING A PEDESTAL SINK

Position a dual-handle faucet as shown above. Assemble the washers and locknuts on the inlet shanks, then tighten the nuts. Remove excess putty from around the faucet. Connect the supply lines to the inlet shanks.

Most single-lever faucets include short supply tubes; simply tighten the locknuts on the threaded stubs from below. For details, see pages 92–93.

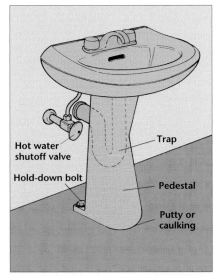

Position the sink on top of the pedestal and, if required by the manufacturer's instructions, bolt the two pieces together as directed.

## INSTALLING A WALL-HUNG SINK

For new installations, you'll need to remove the wallcoverings and drywall. Notch two studs directly behind the sink's proposed location, and nail or screw a 1 by 6 or a 1 by 8 mounting board flush to the stud fronts; then re-cover the wall.

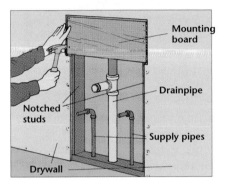

Before you attach the mounting bracket to the wall mounting board, check to see that it fits the sink. Refer to the manufacturer's instructions to position the bracket properly. Generally, you center the bracket over the drainpipe, then level it at the desired height from the floor. Fasten the bracket to the mounting board with wood screws, making sure that it's level. Then carefully lower the sink onto the mounting bracket.

A large wall-hung sink may cause the mounting bracket to bend or even break because of its weight, so the manufacturer may recommend that adjustable legs be inserted into the holes under the front corners of the sink. Screw the legs down until the sink is level, keeping the legs plumb.

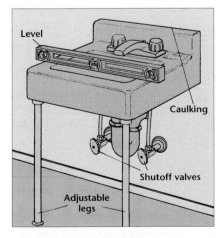

Seal the joint between the back of the sink and the wall with caulking compound.

## INSTALLING A DECK-MOUNT SINK

If your countertop doesn't have a hole for the sink, you'll need to cut one. For a self-rimmed sink, mark the hole, using the templates supplied by the manufacturer with the sink. If you didn't receive a template, cut one from paper; it should fit loosely around the outside of the sink bowl where the bowl meets the flange.

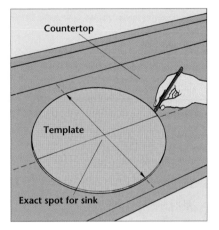

For a rimmed sink, trace the bottom edge of the sink's metal framing rim directly onto the spot where the sink will sit in the countertop.

After you mark the location of the cutout, drill a starting hole, then use a saber saw to cut the opening.

Install your deck-mount sink as described below.

**Self-rimmed sinks.** First, run a bead of caulking compound or plumber's putty around the underside of the flange. Set the sink on the countertop and press it down until the putty oozes out. Install any lugs or clamps according to the manufacturer's instructions. Then carefully remove any excess putty.

**Flush-mount sinks.** Apply a bead of caulking compound or plumber's putty around the sink lip. Fasten the metal framing rim around the lip, following the manufacturer's directions. Next, apply a bead of

caulking compound or plumber's putty around the top edge of the countertop sink opening, and set the sink and rim in place. Secure the sink and rim to the underside of the countertop with the lugs or clamps provided. Wipe off any excess putty.

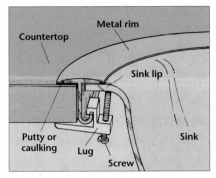

**Undermounted sinks.** For rimless sinks, turn the countertop upside down and apply plumber's putty or caulking compound on the underside, around the edge of the sink opening. Set the sink in place, checking from the other side to be sure it is centered in the opening. Anchor the sink as recommended by the manufacturer. If you're finishing the countertop with ceramic tile, mount the sink atop the plywood base and then edge it with tile trim.

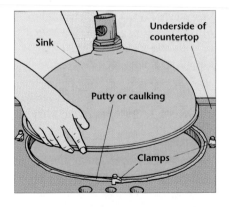

## CONNECTING THE PLUMBING

Once the sink is installed, connect the supply lines to the shutoff valves and tighten the coupling nuts. Connect the trap to the drainpipe and tailpiece. Tighten the slip nuts (see illustration on page 82). Connect the pop-up stopper to the faucet pop-up rod (see page 93). Turn on the water at the shutoff valves or main shutoff, and check for leaks.

Installing or replacing a bathtub can be a complicated job—one that takes careful planning. But a gleaming new tub in your bathroom is well worth the effort.

Your tub choices range from porcelain-enameled cast iron or steel to lightweight fiberglass-reinforced plastic. The waterproof covering around a tub (called a surround) can be tile or fiberglass-reinforced panels or coated hardboard.

If you are building a new bathroom, you can create an entire new bath area with a tub and surround manufactured as a one-piece unit. These units are not recommended for remodeling projects, because they are usually too large to fit through a door and must be moved in before the bathroom walls are framed. When remodeling, your best choice is a tub with separate wall panels or tiles.

Before you install a tub in a new location, check local building codes for support requirements; a bathtub filled with water is extremely heavy and needs plenty of support. Also check the plumbing code requirements for extending the water supply and drain-waste and vent systems (see pages 72–74). You may want to consider getting professional help to build the framing and to rough-in plumbing for a new installation.

This section has directions for removing and installing bathtubs and surrounds. For product information, see page 57.

## REMOVING A BATHTUB

There are three main steps to this job: disconnecting the appropriate plumbing, removing part or all of the wallcovering, and removing the tub itself.

### DISCONNECTING THE PLUMBING

Generally it's not necessary to turn off the water unless you're replacing the faucet body. If you do need to turn off the water, do so at the fixture shutoff valves (if you can reach them through an access door in an adjoining room or hallway) or at the main shutoff valve. Open the faucets to drain the pipes.

Next, remove any fittings—spout, faucet parts, shower head, and diverter handle—that will be in the way. To remove the tub, you'll also have to unscrew and remove the overflow cover and drain lever. By pulling out this fitting, you'll also remove the bathtub drain assembly if it's a trip-lever type.

If you have a pop-up stopper, pull it out with the rocker linkage after removing the overflow cover (see illustration below).

If there's an access door or access from the basement or crawlspace, use a pipe wrench to loosen the coupling nuts from behind the tub; disconnect the trap and waste tee, as shown below, at right. If you can't

get access to the drain plumbing, you can work from inside the tub. Disconnect the tub from the overflow pipe and drainpipe by unscrewing the overflow retainer flange and drain flange.

### REMOVING THE WALL-COVERING

Most bathtubs are recessed; that is, they are surrounded by walls on three sides. Depending on whether you want to replace the tub only, or the tub and the wallcovering, you'll need to remove all or part of the surrounding tiles or panels. Before doing this, remove any fittings, such as the shower head, that are in the way (if you haven't yet done so).

**Tile.** If there are wall or floor tiles along the edge of the tub, free the tub by chipping out approximately 4 inches to the nearest grout joint (see illustration on page 87, top left). On the walls, remove the plaster or drywall backing at the same time, so that several inches of wall studs are exposed. Use a cold chisel and soft-headed steel hammer to remove the tile, and be sure to guard your eyes from fragments by wearing protective goggles.

If you're removing a recessed tub, you must also remove enough tile (and other obstructions) from the floor and walls to be able to slide the tub out of its recess.

**Fiberglass panels.** Take out the wall panels by first removing the drywall or

### DISCONNECTING THE PLUMBING

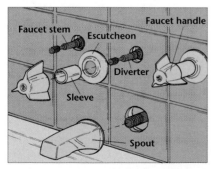

**Remove faucet and diverter parts** and spout, leaving stubout for spout and faucet and diverter stems.

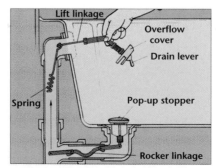

**Unscrew overflow cover,** then pull out drain assembly—first the overflow cover and lift linkage, then the pop-up stopper.

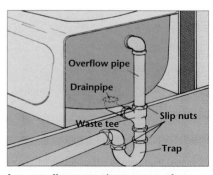

**Loosen slip nuts** and remove trap from underneath tub; then disconnect and remove overflow pipe.

## REMOVING WALLCOVERINGS

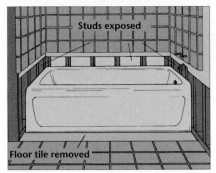

**For tile walls,** chip away at a 4-inch strip of tile and backing from walls; remove an equivalent strip from a tile floor.

molding from the panel flanges. With a pry bar, pry the panels, along with any backing, off the studs. Once the end panels are removed, you can take out the back panel, leaving the exposed wall studs (see illustration, above right).

## REMOVING THE TUB

The tub's bulk will make this one of your biggest jobs. To get the tub out, you may first have to remove the bathroom door or even cut a hole in the wall opposite the tub plumbing. Plan exactly how you'll route the tub through and out of the house. You'll need helpers to move it, especially if it's a heavy steel or cast-iron fixture.

**Steel or cast-iron tubs.** Locate and remove from the wall studs any nails or screws at the top of the tub's flange (lip) that may be holding the tub in place. With at least one helper (probably at least three for a cast-iron tub) lift the tub with a pry bar and slide two or three soaped wooden runners under it (see the illustration at right). Then slide the tub out of the recess.

**Fiberglass tubs.** To remove a fiberglass or plastic tub, pull out all nails or screws driven into the wall studs through the flange. Reach between the studs and grasp the tub under the flange (see illustration far right); with the aid of a helper, if necessary, pull the tub up off its supports and out of the recess.

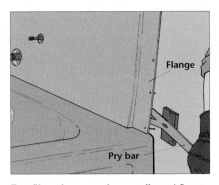

**For fiberglass panels,** pry off panel flange and pull the panel and any backing off the wall studs.

### INSTALLING A BATHTUB

If you're replacing an old tub with a new one, carefully inspect the subfloor where the tub will be installed for level and for moisture damage, and make any necessary repairs or adjustments.

If you're installing a tub in a new location, you'll need to do the framing and rough-in the plumbing first (see "Structural basics," pages 67–70, and "Plumbing basics," pages 72–75).

## SETTING, LEVELING, AND SECURING THE TUB

This is the most crucial part of the installation process. A bathtub must be correctly supported and carefully secured in a level position so that it will drain properly and all plumbing connections can be made easily. Take your time to set and level properly.

### MOVING THE TUB

**To move a steel or cast-iron tub,** slide it across the floor on soaped wooden runners. You'll need several helpers.

**Steel or cast-iron tubs.** These heavy tubs require either vertical or horizontal wood supports (see "Four ways to support a tub" on the following page). Horizontal supports are 1 by 4s or 2 by 4s, nailed across the wall studs so that the tub's flange rests on them. Vertical supports are 2 by 4s nailed to each stud. Position the supports so that the tub will be level both from end to end and from back to front.

If your tub is steel, you can attach prefabricated metal hangers to the studs with wood screws to support the tub.

When you have attached the appropriate supports, slide the new tub along soaped wooden runners into position (see illustration below). With the aid of several helpers, lift it so that the flanges rest on the supports. Check the tub at both ends to see that it's level. If not, insert shims between the tub and wall supports or floor to level it. To prevent the tub from slipping, anchor it by driving nails or screws into the studs tight against the top of the flange.

**Fiberglass tubs.** Temporarily remove any protruding stubouts, if necessary. Then, with a helper, set the tub on the wood supports, placing it tight against the rear studs.

Once the tub is in position, check on top for level at both ends, shimming where needed, as for steel and cast-iron models. Drill holes in the tub flange and carefully nail or screw through the holes into the studs.

**To move a fiberglass tub,** grasp it under the back of the flange and lift it up and out. Having a helper will make the job easier.

## CONNECTING THE PLUMBING

Once the tub is secured in position, reconnect the overflow pipe, the trap, and the drain assembly, being careful not to overtighten the nuts and crack the tub's surface. Make sure that you connect the overflow pipe with the tub drainpipe on the side of the trap that is nearest the bathtub, not on the far side.

If you are reusing the existing wall-coverings, install the faucet and spout, plus a diverter and shower head as required. If you plan on installing a new wallcovering (see below), connect the fittings afterwards.

## INSTALLING THE WALL-COVERING

Before patching or re-covering the walls with either tile or panels, turn on the water and check the drain and supply pipes for leaks.

If you plan to install a tiled wall, see pages 103–105. If you're starting from scratch, it's best to use cement backer board as a base.

To install new fiberglass panels, cover any exposed studs with drywall (cut to accommodate the plumbing) or cement backer board. Then follow the procedure below.

**Drill pipe holes.** To install a fiberglass panel over pipe stubouts and faucet

and diverter stems, you'll need to mark and drill it accurately (see illustration below). Measure and mark the panel by holding it up against the stubouts and stems. Drill slightly oversized holes in the panel with a spade bit, backing the panel with a wood plank to prevent splintering.

**Set panels.** Apply mastic in S-patterns to the backs of the panels (see illustration below), and press the panels in

place around the top of the tub, according to the manufacturer's directions. If panels are to be nailed or screwed to the studs, first drill all nail holes.

**Finish and seal panels.** Seal all the gaps between the wallcovering and the stubouts and stems with silicone caulk. Then attach the faucet and diverter parts, the spout, and the shower head. Allow the silicone caulk to dry before turning on the water.

## FOUR WAYS TO SUPPORT A TUB

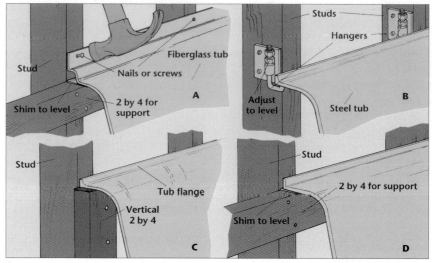

**Support a new tub** in one of these ways: nail or screw fiberglass tub flange to studs (A); support steel tub with metal hangers (B); nail vertical 2 by 4s to studs to support metal tubs (C); nail horizontal 2 by 4s to support metal tubs (D).

## INSTALLING PANELS AROUND A TUB

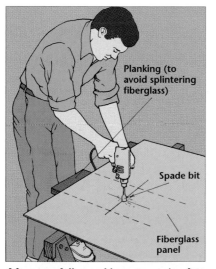

**After carefully marking** one panel to fit over the stubouts and faucet and diverter stems, drill holes in it with a spade bit.

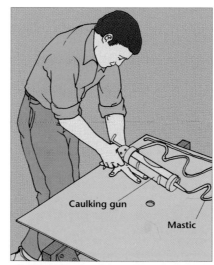

**Apply mastic** to panel in S-patterns while the panel rests on planks laid across a pair of sawhorses.

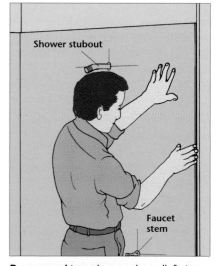

**Press panel** into place on the wall, fitting it over the stubouts and the faucet and diverter stems.

From elegant ceramic tile to easy-to-install fiberglass or plastic panels, your choices are many when it comes to replacing or adding a shower in your home. And if you're installing a completely new bathroom, you can choose a molded one-piece shower enclosure as well. (These are not usually recommended for remodeling projects, because they often won't fit through bathroom doors.)

In this section on showers you will find instructions for removing all types of showers (including the older metal units) and for installing tile and fiberglass-reinforced or plastic-paneled showers. For more details on the various models, see page 58.

## REMOVING A SHOWER

Most showers consist of three walls with a waterproof wallcovering, such as tile or panels, and a separate base, mounted in a wooden frame. Removing a shower is a three-step procedure: disconnecting the plumbing, removing the wallcovering, and removing the base. If the shower is a one-piece unit, you'll also have to cut a hole in a wall to get it out, unless you cut the unit into pieces.

If you're changing the location of a shower or permanently removing it, you'll probably want to dismantle the wood frame and remove the plumbing.

### DISCONNECTING THE PLUMBING

First remove the shower door or the rod and curtain. Then turn off the water supply to the fixture shutoff valves (sometimes accessible through an access door in an adjoining hallway or closet) or at the main shutoff valve. Open the faucets to drain the pipes. Then sponge the shower base dry.

Remove the faucet handles and other trim parts, leaving the faucet stems. Then remove the shower head with a pipe wrench tape-wrapped to avoid scarring the fixture (see illustration above).

## DISCONNECTING SHOWER PLUMBING

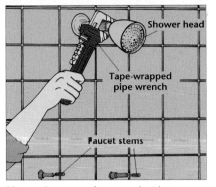

**Use a pipe wrench** wrapped with tape to remove the shower head. (Faucet parts have already been removed.)

Unscrew and pry up the drain cover, and with a pair of pliers and a small pry bar unscrew the crosspiece (see illustration). If you're removing a one-piece shower enclosure, you'll also have to disconnect the drainpipe and remove protruding faucet steps and fittings that might get in the way when you tip the unit to pull it out. Finally, plug the drain opening with a rag to prevent debris from falling into it.

## REMOVING THE WALL-COVERING

The removal procedure you'll follow depends on whether you have a tiled

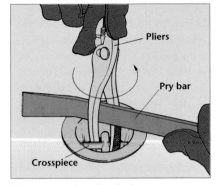

**After removing the drain cover,** use pliers and a pry bar to unscrew the crosspiece from the drain.

shower, walls covered with fiberglass panels, or an older metal shower.

After you've removed the wall-covering, check for moisture damage to the frame and to any soundproofing insulation secured across the inside of the frame. Repair or replace if necessary.

**Tile.** Ceramic tile is the most difficult wallcovering to remove. If the existing tile is clean, smooth, and securely attached, you can avoid removing it by using it as a backing for a new tile surface. If you must remove it, proceed with caution and wear goggles and gloves while you work.

## REMOVING SHOWER WALLS

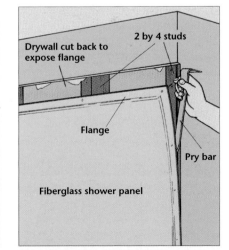

**For tile walls,** chip and pry off tile and drywall backing to expose the entire frame of the shower.

**For panel walls,** remove any drywall or molding covering panel flanges; then pry the panels off the frame.

To remove tile set in mortar, you must break up the tile, mortar, and any backing with a sledgehammer. Remove it down to the wood frame, being careful not to hit and possibly damage the wall studs. You may want to hire a tile professional for this part of the project.

If the tile is set on drywall with adhesive, use a cold chisel and ball-peen hammer, wearing gloves and goggles, to chip away small sections of tile and backing. Then insert a pry bar and pry off large sections of tile and backing until the entire frame is exposed (see illustration, page 89).

**Fiberglass panels.** First remove any molding or drywall covering and panel flanges. Then pry panels, along with any backing and nails, off the wood frame (see illustration, page 89). If you're removing a one-piece enclosure, you may have to cut it apart to get it out (a saber saw with a plastic-cutting blade will do the job quickly).

**Metal showers.** Remove metal shower walls by unscrewing them at the edges and then at the front and back corners. These screws hold the shower walls to each other and sometimes to a wood frame. If the screws are rusted, cut the screw heads off with a hacksaw or cold chisel; then separate the walls with a hard pull.

### REMOVING THE BASE

The base may be tile on a mortar bed, or it may be a fiberglass unit. Tile is difficult to remove because it's laid in mortar; fiberglass bases can be easily pried out.

After you've removed the base, inspect the subfloor and framing for moisture damage, and repair wherever it is necessary.

**Tile on mortar.** As with tile walls, check first to see if you can lay the new tile over the old. If not, use a sledgehammer to break up and remove all tile and mortar down to the subfloor. You may be able to pry up one side of the base and slip a wedge under it to make it easier to break up. Always

wear goggles to protect your eyes from tile or mortar fragments.

**Fiberglass.** Remove all nails or screws from the flange around the top of the base. Pry the base off the floor with a prybar; lift it out.

Nails removed from flange

Pry bar

### INSTALLING A SHOWER

When you replace an old shower, the plumbing—and probably the wood frame—will already be in place.

If you're putting a shower in a new location, you must first frame the shower walls using 2 by 4s (see "Structural basics," pages 67–70). Make accurate measurements and keep the framing square and plumb. (Follow the manufacturer's directions to frame a fiberglass shower.)

Once the frame is complete, you'll also need to rough-in the supply and drain lines, and install the faucet and pipe for the shower head (see pages 72–75 and 94).

Now you are ready to install the shower—first the base, then the walls.

### INSTALLING THE BASE

Installing a watertight tiled base on a mortar bed is a highly complicated project not recommended for beginners. If you want this type of base in either a tile or panel shower, consider having a professional build it.

To install a fiberglass or plastic base, position it over the drain outlet. Connect the base to the drain by screwing in the crosspiece (see illustration,

page 89), and cover the opening with rags to keep debris from falling in. Follow the manufacturer's directions to secure the base to the frame (nailing is shown below). Later, remove the rags and attach the drain cover.

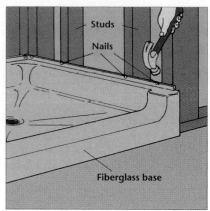
Studs

Nails

Fiberglass base

### INSTALLING THE WALL-COVERING

Once the base is secured, you're ready to cover the shower's side and back walls with tile or panels.

**Tile.** Like a tile base, tile walls can be tricky to install. If you want tile on a mortar bed, you may want to hire a tile contractor to install it. If you are planning to back the tile with either drywall or cement backer board, you may decide to do the job yourself.

First, prepare the backing. Cut holes for the shower head stubout and faucet stems; then nail the backing to the frame (see illustration page 91, top left).

Plan the layout of your tile by marking horizontal and vertical working lines on the shower wall (see illustrations on page 91, top middle). Using thin-set adhesive, set tiles on the back wall first. Then move on to the sides, cutting tiles to fit around the shower stubout and faucet stems.

Set ceramic tile accessories. Allow the tile to set (for the required time, consult the adhesive manufacturer's instructions) before grouting all the joints between tiles. When the grout has set, you can seal it. For more information on establishing working lines, setting tile, and grouting joints, turn to pages 103-105; or consult your tile dealer.

## INSTALLING TILE ON SHOWER WALLS

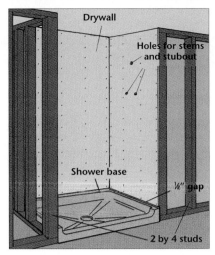

**To attach drywall** or backer board to a wood shower frame, nail along the length of the 2 by 4 studs.

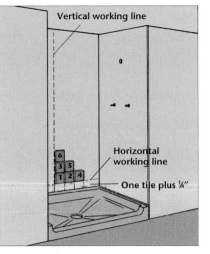

**Mark working lines,** both horizontal and vertical, then set tile on shower walls in a pyramid fashion.

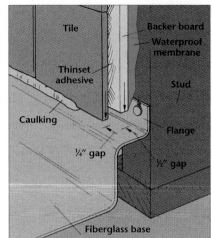

**Backing is positioned** to leave ½-inch gap above base; leave ¼-inch gap for caulking tile.

**Fiberglass panels.** Shower panels of fiberglass usually come with manufacturer's directions for installation. Some require no backing (except perhaps soundproofing insulation); others require a backing of backer board and a waterproof membrane.

For both types of panels, measure and mark on one panel the locations of the shower head stubout and the faucet stems. Lay the marked panel carefully across two sawhorses, and with a spade bit, drill slightly over-sized holes for your fittings. Support the panels with wood planks so you

don't splinter them as you drill (see the illustration below).

If the base of your shower has channels on the outside edges for sealant, clean out any debris from them. Then fill the groove at the back with the sealant recommended by the manufacturer (see illustration below). Also apply adhesive to the reverse side of the back panel according to manufacturer's directions.

Install the back panel by fitting it into the groove on the base, then pressing it against the frame to make a complete seal. Next, fill the other

grooves on the base with sealant and install the side panels; they may snap or clip to the back panel. Screw or nail the flanges of the panels to the framing. Install cover moldings over the nails or screws, if required.

## CONNECTING THE PLUMBING

Once you've installed the wall coverings, caulk around all openings; then re-attach the shower head, escutcheons, and the faucet handles.

Finally, hang the shower door, or install hardware and a curtain rod, and hang a shower curtain.

## INSTALLING FIBERGLASS SHOWER PANELS

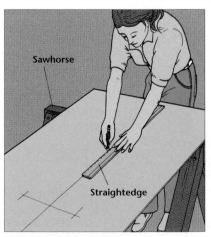

**Mark a panel** for stubout hole and faucet stem, set panel on supporting planks and sawhorses, and drill holes.

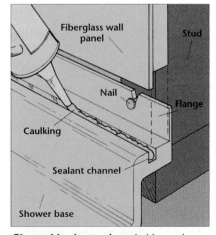

**Channel in shower base** holds panel tightly in place; sealant prevents moisture from getting behind panels.

**Press panel to the frame,** guiding head stubout and faucet stems through holes; nail or screw panel flange to frame.

Whether you're replacing an old faucet or selecting fittings for a new sink or bathtub, you'll find a wide variety of faucet types and styles from which to choose. The product information on page 59 can help you make your selection.

In this section, you'll find information on removing and installing two different types of widely used bathroom faucets: deck-mount models for sinks, and wall-mount models for bathtubs and showers.

## SINK FAUCETS

In choosing a deck-mount faucet, be sure that the faucet's inlet shanks are spaced to fit the holes in your sink. If you are replacing a faucet, it's wise to take the old one with you when you shop. You'll also need new water supply lines, so take them with you, too.

Choose a unit that comes with clear installation instructions, and make sure that repair kits or replacement parts are readily available.

### REMOVING A SINK FAUCET

Before removing the faucet, turn off the water at the sink shutoff valves or main shutoff valve. Place a bucket under the valves and use a wrench to remove the coupling nuts connecting water supply lines to the valves. Open the faucet and allow the water to drain from the lines.

If your sink has a pop-up drain, you'll need to disconnect it before removing the faucet. Unfasten the clevis screw and spring clip that secure the pivot rod to the pop-up rod, and remove the pop-up rod from the faucet body (see illustration on facing page).

With an adjustable wrench or basin wrench, reach up behind the sink and remove the coupling nuts holding the supply lines to the inlet shanks on the faucet (see illustration above). Use the wrench to remove the locknuts from the shanks. Take off the washers; then lift up the faucet and remove it from the sink or countertop.

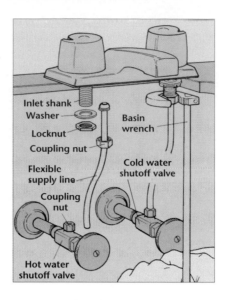

### INSTALLING A SINK FAUCET

Before you begin, have an adjustable wrench on hand. If your new faucet does not come with a rubber gasket, you will also need to have a supply of plumber's putty.

If you're installing a new faucet on an old sink, clean the area around the faucet to make sure it is free of dirt and any mineral buildup.

The basic steps in installing a sink faucet are outlined below, but since procedures vary with the type of faucet, you should also look carefully at the manufacturer's instructions.

**Mounting the faucet.** If your new faucet doesn't have a rubber gasket on the bottom, apply a bead of plumber's putty around the underside of the outside edge.

The faucet may have either inlet shanks or inlet tubes and threaded mounting studs. Insert the inlet shanks or tubes down through the holes in the mounting surface; press the faucet into the surface. For a faucet with inlet shanks, screw the washers and locknuts onto the shanks by hand (see illustration, below left); tighten with a wrench. If your faucet has tubes, assemble and tighten the washers and nuts on mounting studs (see illustration, below right).

**Connecting the plumbing.** Two types of flexible supply lines are available: chrome-plated corrugated metal tubing and plastic tubing. Because it's a little better looking, metal tubing is usually used when the supply lines are visible. Gaskets and coupling nuts for it are sold separately, so be sure they fit the faucet and the shutoff valves. Plastic tubing is sold with gaskets and coupling nuts already assembled.

Before connecting the supply lines, apply pipe joint compound to the threads on the inlet shanks and shutoff valves, or to the threads on the fittings at the ends of the tubing.

### INSTALLING A SINGLE-LEVER FAUCET

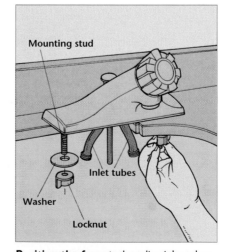

**Position the faucet,** threading inlet tubes through the sink hole; then tighten the locknuts on the mounting studs.

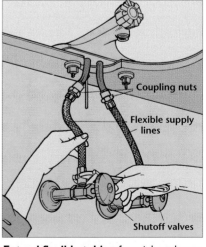

**Extend flexible tubing** from inlet tubes as required; attach it to shutoff valves with an adjustable wrench.

Then connect the supply lines to the inlet shanks or tubes (see illustration page 92, bottom right). Tighten the coupling nuts with a wrench. Gently bend the supply lines to meet the shutoff valves, and secure them to the valves with coupling nuts. Tighten the nuts with an adjustable wrench, then turn on the water and check for leaks.

If you're installing a new pop-up drain assembly, follow the instructions from the manufacturer. Connect the pop-up rod to the new pivot rod, using the fastenings supplied with the new drain assembly.

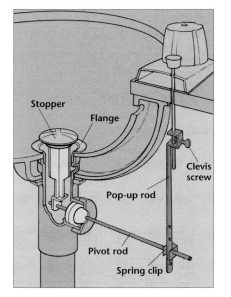

Stopper
Flange
Clevis screw
Pop-up rod
Pivot rod
Spring clip

**TWO TYPES OF BATHTUB AND SHOWER FAUCETS**

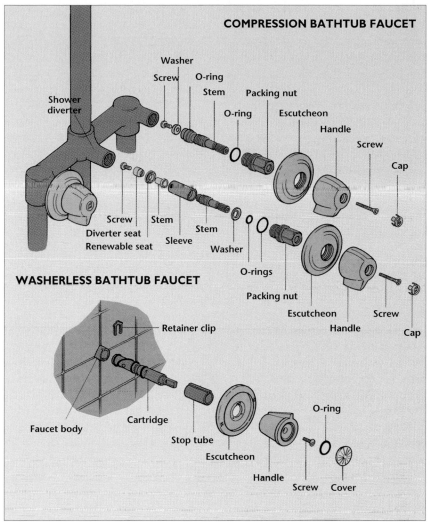

COMPRESSION BATHTUB FAUCET

Washer
Screw
O-ring
Stem
Packing nut
Shower diverter
O-ring
Escutcheon
Handle
Screw
Cap

Screw
Stem
Diverter seat
Renewable seat
Sleeve
Stem
Washer
O-rings
Packing nut
Escutcheon
Handle
Screw
Cap

WASHERLESS BATHTUB FAUCET

Retainer clip
Faucet body
Cartridge
Stop tube
Escutcheon
Handle
Screw
Cover
O-ring

## TUB AND SHOWER FAUCETS

Faucets for bathtubs and showers are either compression models (usually with separate hot and cold water controls) or washerless models (with a single lever or knob to control the flow and mix of hot and cold water). In both types (see illustration, above right), the faucet body is mounted directly on the water supply pipes inside the wall.

You can either renovate a bathtub or shower faucet, or completely replace it. If the faucet body is in good condition, you may simply want to replace some of the faucet parts. If the faucet body is in poor condition, or if you want to change the type of faucet you have, you may have to replace the entire assembly. You'll also need to re-

place the complete faucet if you want to add a shower head above an existing bathtub (see "Adding a shower faucet," page 94). The following sections tell you how to renovate or replace a faucet.

### RENOVATING A BATHTUB OR SHOWER FAUCET

To renovate a faucet, you can replace faucet parts—stems, handles, and trim (such as escutcheons)—and the tub spout or shower head. In a tub, you might also replace the diverter—the mechanism that redirects water to the shower pipe. To find the correct replacement parts, it's a good idea to disassemble the old faucet first, then take the parts with you to the store when you shop for new ones.

Before you start work, turn off the water at the bathtub or shower shutoff

valves or at the main shutoff valve. (Bathtub or shower shutoff valves may be accessible through a panel in an adjoining room, hall, or closet.)

The drawings on this page show you how typical compression and washerless faucets are put together, but the actual assembly you have may vary with individual models. As you disassemble your faucet, take notes and make a sketch of the parts and the sequence of assembly so you'll be able to put the faucet back together. First remove faucet handles, trim, and stem parts; then take out the diverter (if necessary). Finally, remove the tub spout or shower head with a tape-wrapped pipe wrench.

When you're ready to assemble the new fittings, you can simply reverse the procedure.

## REMOVING A BATHTUB FAUCET

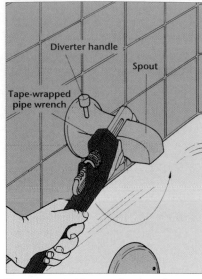

**Remove spout** from wall stubout by turning counterclockwise with a tape-wrapped pipe wrench.

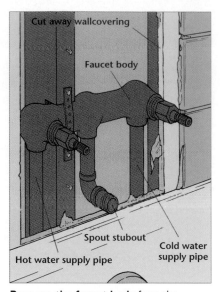

**Remove the faucet body** from the supply pipes by unscrewing or unsoldering the connections.

## REPLACING A BATHTUB OR SHOWER FAUCET

Replacing a complete bathtub or shower faucet involves cutting away the wall-covering and removing the faucet body from the supply pipes with wrenches or a small propane torch. You'll need to take the old faucet body with you when you buy a new one, to be sure of getting the correct size. If you've never done any pipefitting, you may want to get professional help to install the new faucet body.

**Getting to the faucet body.** First remove the faucet handles and trim, plus the shower head or tub spout and diverter. To work on the faucet body and the pipes behind the wall, open the access door or panel if one is available. If not, cut a hole in the bathroom wall large enough to allow you to work on the faucet body and pipes comfortably (see illustration at right). Then turn off the water at the bathtub shutoff valves or main shutoff valve.

**Removing the faucet body.** The illustration above shows how a bathtub or shower faucet body is mounted onto the water supply pipes. It may be attached with either threaded or soldered connections. If you should find threaded

connections, unscrew them. Use one wrench on the supply pipe to hold it steady and a second wrench on the coupling, turning it counterclockwise. If you find soldered copper connections, unsolder them, using a small propane torch. Use metal or asbestos shields to protect the framing from fire.

**Installing the faucet body.** If your tub or shower is not equipped with individual shutoff valves, you may want to add them now (or consult a professional plumber for help). To install a faucet body on threaded pipe fittings, apply pipe joint compound to the male threads of the pipes and screw the connecting coupling nuts down tight.

For copper pipe, solder couplings to the pipes and screw them onto the faucet body. If the faucet body must be soldered directly to the pipe, first remove the valve and diverter stems.

After the pipes are connected to the faucet body, turn the water on and check for leaks. To make certain that the pipes can't vibrate when the water is turned on and off, anchor them and the faucet body firmly to the wall studs, or support them with pipe straps before patching and re-covering the wall.

Carefully measure and mark the positions of the new faucet, spout, and

shower head stubouts on the replacement wallcovering. Then prepare and replace the wallcoverings and attach the new fittings.

## ADDING A SHOWER FAUCET

To add a shower head above your old bathtub, you'll have to replace the old faucet assembly with one equipped with a shower outlet and diverter valve. In addition, you'll have to install a shower pipe in the wall, as shown below.

If your tub surround is tiled, the tile will have to be removed so you can add the shower pipe. Cut your access hole large enough to install the shower pipe. From the shower outlet on the faucet body, run a ½-inch pipe up the wall to the desired height (see illustration, page 75) and top it with an elbow. Nail a 2 by 4 wood support behind the elbow and anchor the pipe to it with a pipe strap.

To avoid scratching the shower arm while you're repairing the wall covering, thread a 6-inch galvanized nipple onto the elbow in place of the shower arm.

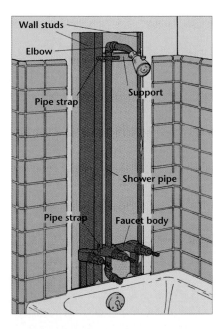

Finally, clean the pipe threads and install the shower arm and shower head, using pipe joint compound on the male threads of the fittings. Repair or replace wallcoverings as required (see pages 98–105).

Removing or installing a toilet is not very complicated, especially when the plumbing is already in place. During major remodeling involving the floor or walls, remember that toilets (and bidets) are the first fixtures to remove and the last to install.

For product information on various toilet models, see page 60.

Conventional two-piece toilets have a floor-mounted bowl with a tank mounted on the bowl. Older types with floor-mounted bowls may have the tank mounted on the wall. One-piece toilets, with the bowl and tank mounted on the floor as a single unit, are becoming as popular with homeowners as two-piece models. (One-piece wall-hung models that connect directly to the stack in the wall are also available.) This section deals primarily with conventional floor-mounted toilets.

Before you begin work, be sure to check any code requirements for a new or replacement toilet.

## REMOVING A TOILET

The procedure for removing a toilet varies with the type of fixture. For a two-piece toilet, you remove the tank first, then the bowl. (For a one-piece toilet, you remove the tank and bowl at the same time.)

## DISCONNECT WATER SUPPLY

Before you begin work, turn off the water at the fixture shutoff valve or main shutoff valve. Flush the toilet twice to empty the bowl and tank; then sponge out any remaining water. To remove the toilet seat and lid, unfasten the nuts on the two bolts projecting down through the bowl's back edge. Unfasten the coupling nuts on the water supply line (see illustration, below left) underneath the tank. If the line is kinked or corroded, replace it when you install the new toilet.

## REMOVE THE TANK

If you're removing a bowl-mounted toilet tank, detach the empty tank from the bowl as follows. Locate the mounting bolts inside the tank at the bottom. Hold them stationary with a screwdriver while you use a wrench to unfasten the nuts underneath the tank (see illustration, below). You'll find it easier to remove the nuts if a helper holds the screwdriver. Then lift up the tank and remove it.

## REMOVE THE BOWL

The following instructions apply to most floor-mounted toilet bowls. At the base of the bowl near the floor, pry off the caps covering the hold-down floor bolts. Unscrew the nuts from the

bolts. If the nuts have rusted on, soak them with penetrating oil or cut the bolts off with a hacksaw.

Gently rock the bowl from side to side, breaking the seal between the bowl and the floor. Lift the bowl straight up, keeping it level so any remaining water doesn't spill from its trap (see illustration, below).

Stuff a rag into the open drainpipe to prevent sewer gas from escaping and to keep debris from falling into the opening while you get ready to install the new toilet.

## INSTALLING A TOILET

The amount of work needed to install a new toilet depends on whether it will be in a new location. Hooking up a toilet in a new spot is a challenging project, because you must extend supply, drain, and vent pipes (see pages 72–75). You may want to have a professional run the piping to the desired spot and then complete the installation yourself.

Replacing an old fixture with a new one at the same location is a one-afternoon project that you can do yourself. The only crucial dimension you need to check on a new toilet is its roughing-in size—the distance from the wall to the center of the drainpipe. Rough-in sizes are usually 12 inches.

### REMOVING A FLOOR-MOUNTED TOILET

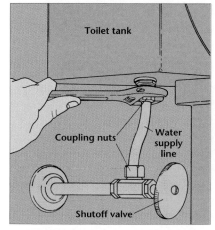

**Loosen the coupling nut** on the water supply line at the bottom of the tank using a wrench.

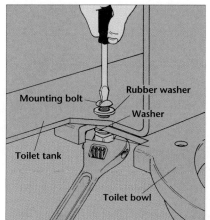

**Detach the tank** from the bowl by loosening the mounting bolts with a screwdriver and a wrench.

**Lift the bowl** straight up off the floor flange, keeping it level to avoid spilling any remaining water.

You can usually determine the roughing-in size before removing the old bowl. Just measure from the wall to one of the two hold-down bolts that secure the bowl to the floor. (If the bowl has four such bolts, measure to one of the rear bolts.) Your new toilet's roughing-in size can be shorter than that of the fixture you're replacing, but if it's longer the new toilet won't fit.

Once you've determined that the fixture will fit, you're ready to install it.

The following general instructions apply to two-piece floor-mounted toilets. The key steps are illustrated on page 97. (For a one-piece, floor-mounted toilet, install the bowl as described below, then connect the water supply.)

# The inner workings of a toilet

There are two systems under a toilet tank lid: an inlet-valve assembly, which regulates the filling of the tank, and a flush valve assembly, which controls the flow of water from the tank into the bowl.

When you press the flush handle on the toilet, the trip lever raises the lift rod wires (or chain) connected to the tank stopper. As the stopper goes up, water rushes into the bowl. Because of gravity, the water goes out the trap and to the drainpipe.

Once the tank empties, the stopper drops and the float ball or cup trips the inlet-valve assembly to let fresh water into the tank. While the tank is filling, some of the water is allowed into the bowl; this water seals the trap. As the water level in the tank rises, the float ball or cup shuts off the flow of water and the flush is complete.

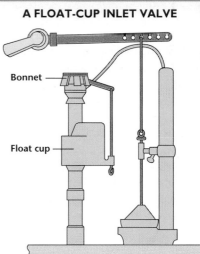

**A FLOAT-CUP INLET VALVE**

Bonnet

Float cup

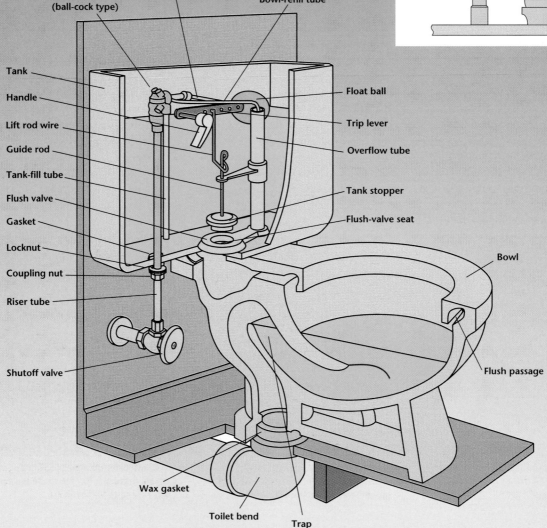

Inlet valve (ball-cock type)
Float arm
Bowl-refill tube
Tank
Handle
Lift rod wire
Guide rod
Tank-fill tube
Flush valve
Gasket
Locknut
Coupling nut
Riser tube
Shutoff valve
Float ball
Trip lever
Overflow tube
Tank stopper
Flush-valve seat
Bowl
Flush passage
Wax gasket
Toilet bend
Trap

## PREPARE THE FLOOR FLANGE

This fitting connects the bowl to the floor and drainpipe.

With a putty knife, scrape off the wax bowl ring that formed the seal between the bowl and the flange. Scrape the flange thoroughly so that the new ring will form a true leakproof seal. Remove the rags from the drain.

If the old flange is cracked or broken, or if its surface is rough, replace it with a new flange, matched to the existing drainpipe material. (Use a plastic flange with plastic pipe, cast iron with a cast iron pipe.) Remove the old hold-down bolts from the floor flange, then insert the new bolts through the flange. If necessary, hold them upright temporarily with plumber's putty. Align the bolts with the center of the drainpipe.

## INSTALL THE BOWL RING

Turn the new bowl upside down on a cushioned surface. Place the new bowl ring over the toilet horn (outlet) on the bottom of the bowl, and apply plumber's putty around the bowl's bottom edge.

## PLACE THE BOWL

Check that all packing material has been removed from the new bowl, and all rags from the drainpipe. Then gently lower the bowl into place over the flange, using the bolts as guides. To form the seal, press down firmly while twisting slightly.

Check the bowl with a level—from side to side and from front to back; use copper or brass washers to shim underneath the bowl where necessary. Be careful not to break the seal. Hand tighten the washers and nuts into the hold-down bolts; you'll tighten them permanently after the tank is in place.

## ATTACH THE TANK

For a bowl-mounted tank, fit the rubber gasket over the end of the flush valve that projects through the bottom of the tank. Place the rubber tank cushion on the rear of the bowl. After positioning the tank on the bowl, insert the mounting bolts through their holes in the bottom of the tank so they

pass through the tank cushion and the back of the bowl. Then tighten the nuts and washers onto the bolts. (Secure wall-mounted tanks to hanger brackets with bolts through the back of the tank. Assemble the large pipe between bowl and tank and tighten the coupling.)

Now you can attach the bowl to the floor permanently. Use a wrench to tighten the hold-down nuts alternately at the base of the bowl, but be sure that you don't overtighten them or you could crack the toilet bowl. Check to see that the bowl is still level and does not rock. Fill the caps with plumber's putty and place them over the nuts. Seal the joint between the base of the bowl and

the floor with a thin bead of caulking compound. Next, attach the toilet seat by inserting the mounting bolts through the holes in the back of the bowl; then assemble the washers and the nuts onto the bolts and tighten them. Check that the seat moves up and down freely.

## CONNECT THE PLUMBING

Now you are ready to connect the water supply line to the underside of the toilet tank. If your old plumbing did not have a fixture shutoff valve, it's a good idea to install one now. (It's worth consulting a professional plumber for help in installing one.) Finally, turn on the water and check for leaks.

## INSTALLING A FLOOR-MOUNTED TOILET

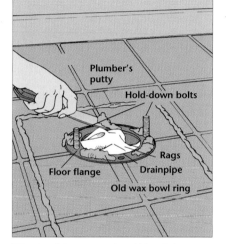

**Thoroughly scrape** the old bowl ring from the floor flange, using a putty knife or similar tool.

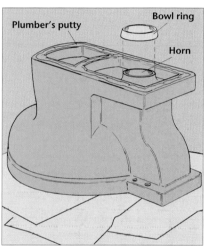

**Position the new bowl ring** over the toilet horn on the bottom of the bowl as it rests on a cushioned surface.

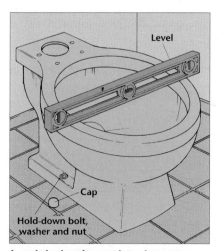

**Level the bowl** once it's in place, using small copper or brass washers to shim underneath if necessary.

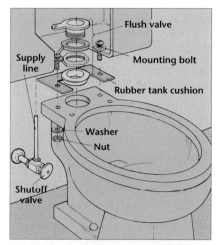

**Attach the tank** to the bowl using the mounting bolts, with the rubber gasket and tank cushion in place.

A new moisture-resistant wall or ceiling can improve the bathroom's appearance and at the same time make the room easier to maintain.

This section will show you how to remove old walls and ceilings and apply the most popular wall treatments in today's bathrooms—drywall, wallpaper, and ceramic tile. (For information on painting, see the special feature on page 102.)

## DRYWALL

Drywall, also called gypsum wallboard, is a versatile wallcovering that has a gypsum core faced with thick paper. You can use it as finish material, painting or wallpapering over it, or you can use it as a backing for other materials, such as tile, wood, or panels of plastic-coated hardboard.

A special water-resistant grade is available for use around tubs, showers, and other areas that get damp. This drywall is usually identified by a blue or green paper cover. It's not a good idea to use it where you plan to paint the drywall or apply wallpaper, because the compound you must use to finish joints between panels of water-resistant drywall is nearly impossible to sand, so every imperfection will show.

Panels are generally 4 feet wide and 8 feet long. (Lengths over 8 feet can be specially ordered.) The common thicknesses are ⅜ inch for drywall used as a

### INSTALLING DRYWALL ON A WALL

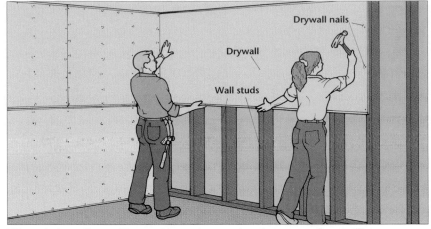

**Lift each drywall panel** into position and center the edges over wall studs. Then nail or screw the panel to the studs, taking care not to puncture the surface of the drywall. Stagger panels in adjacent rows so that the ends don't line up.

backing and ½ inch for drywall used as finish wallcovering.

### REMOVING DRYWALL

If your bathroom's existing drywall has only minor cracks or holes, you can probably repair it by filling in the cracks with ready-mixed spackling compound, then sanding it smooth. But if it's wet, mildewed, or badly damaged, you will have to remove it before installing other wallcovering.

Use a broad-bladed pry bar and a claw hammer to remove drywall. Wear a dust mask to avoid inhaling gypsum dust, and cover all fixtures and the floor with drop cloths. Finally, be sure to turn off electrical power to the bathroom by

flipping a circuit breaker or removing a fuse, so you won't risk hitting a live wire with the pry bar.

Your drywall is probably nailed or screwed at intervals along the wall studs. The removal procedure is similar for either type of fastener.

Break through a taped seam between panels with the pry bar. Then pry up the panel, using the stud for leverage, until you loosen a large piece. With both hands, pull the piece of drywall off the studs. Continue removing large pieces.

Once you've completely stripped the drywall away from the studs, work through the area a second time and pull out any remaining nails. If the drywall is attached with screws, you may be able to

### CUTTING DRYWALL

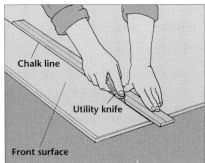

**Cut drywall along the pencil** or chalk line marked on the front face, using a utility knife guided by a straightedge.

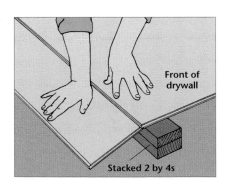

**Break the gypsum core** by placing the edges of stacked 2 by 4s under the cut and pressing down on the panel.

**Complete the cut by turning** the panel over, bending the drywall back, and cutting through the back paper with a utility knife.

## INSTALLING DRYWALL ON A CEILING

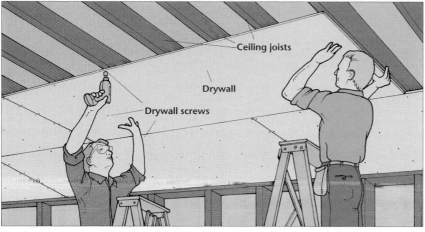

Labels in illustration: Ceiling joists · Drywall · Drywall screws

**It takes two to install a drywall ceiling.** Prop each panel in place with your heads; screw or nail first in the center and then where it will take the weight off your heads. Or rent a drywall jack and use it to raise the panels.

expose enough of the heads so they can be unscrewed. If not, cut the screws flush with the studs using a reciprocating saw or hacksaw.

## INSTALLING DRYWALL

Installing drywall is a three-step procedure. You measure and cut panels to size, hang them, and finish the seams and corners with drywall compound and tape. Handle bulky panels carefully; take care not to bend or break the corners or tear the paper covers.

Installing drywall on the ceiling is basically the same as for walls. If you're covering both the walls and the ceiling, do the ceiling first.

**Cut the drywall.** Though you'll use some full-size panels, you'll also need to cut pieces to fit around obstacles such as doors, windows, fixtures, and cabinets.

To make a straight cut, first mark a line on the front of the panel with a pencil and straightedge, or snap a chalk line. Cut through the front paper with a utility knife, using a straightedge as a guide. Break the gypsum core by bending the board toward the back, as shown in the illustration on page 98 (center, bottom). Finally, cut the paper on the back along the bend. Smooth the cut edge with a perforated rasp.

To fit drywall around doors, windows, and other openings, measure and mark carefully. Measure from the vertical edges of the opening to the edge of the nearest panel or a corner, then measure from the horizontal edges to the floor. Transfer these measurements to the drywall and make the cutout with a keyhole saw. For mid-panel cutouts, drill a pilot hole, then use a keyhole saw to make the cutout.

**Basic wall application.** Wall panels may be positioned either vertically or horizontally—that is, with the long edges either parallel or perpendicular to wall studs. Most professionals prefer the latter method, because it helps bridge irregularities between studs and results in a stronger wall. But if your wall is higher than 8 feet, you may not want to use this method, since the extra height requires more cutting and creates too many joints. Before installing the wall panels, carefully mark the stud locations on the floor and on the ceiling.

Starting at a corner, place the first panel tight against the ceiling and secure it with nails, drywall screws, or construction adhesive supplemented by nails. Drive in the nails with a hammer, dimpling the drywall surface without puncturing the paper. Screws are quick and strong. You will need a power screw gun or a drill with an adjustable clutch to drive them. Fastener spacing is subject to local codes, but typical nail spacing is every 8 inches along ends and edges and along inter-mediate supports (called "in the field"). Typical screw spacing is every 7 inches along panel ends and at the intermediate joists.

Apply additional panels the same way. If you're applying drywall horizontally, stagger the end joints in the bottom row so they don't line up with the joints in the top row.

**Basic ceiling application.** Fasten the panels perpendicular to the joists with annular ring nails, drywall screws, or a combination of nails and construction adhesive.

Because you'll need to support the heavy panels with your head while fastening them, installing a drywall ceiling is a two-person job. First, secure each panel at the center with nails or screws; then place the next few fasteners where they'll take the weight off your heads (see illustration above).

**Tape the joints and corners.** If your drywall will be a backing for paneling, you won't need to tape and conceal the joints or corners. But if you are painting, wallpapering, or installing tile, you must finish the drywall carefully. You will need these basic tools and materials: 6-inch and 10-inch taping knives, a corner tool, sandpaper, drywall tape, and taping compound. (Water-resistant drywall requires a water-resistant compound. See the NOTE on page 100 for taping water-resistant drywall.)

Finishing is done in stages over a period of days. To tape a joint between panels, first apply a smooth layer of taping compound over the joint with a 6-inch taping knife (see illustrations on page 100). Before the compound dries, use the knife to embed drywall tape into it; apply a thin coat of compound over the tape, smoothing it gently with the knife.

Tape and finish all joints between panels in the same manner. Then, with smooth, even strokes of the 6-inch knife, cover the nail dimples in the field with compound.

Allow the taping compound to dry for at least 24 hours, then sand it lightly until it's smooth. Always wear

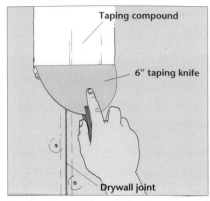

**Apply a smooth layer** of taping compound over the drywall joint, using a 6-inch taping knife.

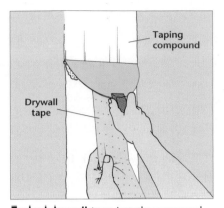

**Embed drywall tape** into the compound before it dries, and apply another thin layer of compound.

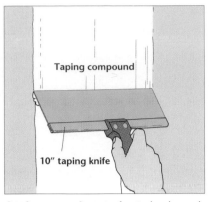

**Apply a second coat** a few inches beyond each side of the joint, feathering the compound out to the edges.

a face mask and goggles, and make sure the room is well ventilated.

Now use a 10-inch knife to apply a second coat of compound, extending it a few inches on each side of the taped joint, feathering the compound out toward the edges.

Let the second coat dry, sand it, then apply a final coat. Use the 10-inch knife to smooth out and feather the edges, covering all dimples and joints. Once the compound dries, sand it again to remove any imperfections, even minor ones.

NOTE: To finish water-resistant drywall that will be the backing for ceramic tile, first embed the tape in water-resistant taping compound along panel joints; then remove all excess compound with a taping knife. Apply a second thin coat over the wet taping coat and fill any nail dimples. Do not leave excess compound—it can't be sanded dry.

To tape an inside corner, use precreased tape. Apply a smooth layer of compound to the drywall on either side of the corner. Measure and tear the tape, fold it in half vertically along the prepared crease, and press it into the corner with a taping knife or corner tool. Apply a thin layer of compound over the tape and smooth it out; then finish the joint.

Now you're ready to nail metal corner beads to all exterior corners to protect them. Apply compound to each side of the corner with a 6-inch knife. When it's dry, sand it smooth.

With a 10-inch knife, apply a second coat of compound, feathering it. Allow to dry, then sand away imperfections.

**Textured versus smooth.** Though many people prefer a smooth look, texture can hide a less-than-perfect taping job—and add a bit of visual interest to a wall as well. Some joint compounds double as texturing compounds; other effects may require special texturing materials. Ask your dealer for advice.

Professionals often apply texturing with a spray gun, but others produce good results by daubing, swirling, or splattering the compound with a sponge, paint roller, or stiff brush—use whatever tool that works to produce the look you want.

Let the compound set up until slightly stiff; then even it out as required with a wide float or trowel. Allow the finished surface to dry for at least 24 hours before painting.

## HANGING NEW WALLPAPER

Next to paint, wallpaper is the most popular covering for bathroom walls.

**Choices.** Wallpaper for the bathroom should be scrubbable, durable, and stain resistant. Solid vinyl wallpapers are a good choice. Vinyl coatings give wallpaper a washable surface but aren't notably durable or grease resistant. If you're a beginner, consider prepasted and pretrimmed paper. To find the right adhesive, check the manufacturer's instructions or ask your dealer.

**Preparing the surface.** Remove all light fixtures and faceplates. Clean and rinse the surface. Remove any old wallpaper before hanging a non-porous covering like solid vinyl.

If the existing paper is strippable, it will come off easily when you pull it up. To remove nonstrippable paper, use a steamer (available for rent) or a spray bottle filled with very hot water. Before steaming, break the surface of the old paper by sanding it with coarse sandpaper or by pulling a sawblade or utility knife across it.

Within a few minutes of steaming (longer if it's nonporous), begin to remove the old paper. Using a broad knife, work down from the top of the wall, scraping off the old wallpaper.

On new drywall, tape all joints between panels before papering. When dry, sand the wall smooth and apply a coat of flat, oil-based primer-sealer.

To apply wallpaper over previously painted surfaces that are in good condition, clean off all the dirt and grease, then let it dry. If latex paint was used, or if you don't know the type, apply an oil-based undercoat over the old paint.

**To begin.** Plan the best place to hang your first strip. If you're papering all four walls with a patterned paper, the last strip you hang probably won't match the first, so plan to start and finish in the least conspicuous place—usually a corner, entry door casing, or window casing.

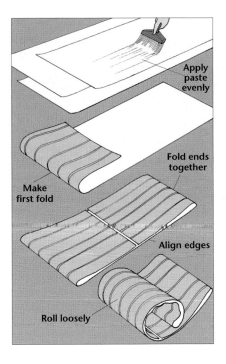

Apply paste evenly

Make first fold

Fold ends together

Align edges

Roll loosely

Most house walls are not straight, so you'll need to establish a plumb line. Figure the width of your first strip of wallpaper minus ½ inch (which will overlap the corner or casing); measure that distance from your starting point, and mark the wall. With a carpenter's level as a straightedge, draw a plumb line through your mark and extend it from floor to ceiling.

Measure the wall height before cutting each strip. Allow 2 inches extra at the top and bottom. Also be sure to allow for any pattern match. Cut the strips with a razor knife. Then number them on the back at the top edge so you can apply them in the proper sequence.

With some wallpapers, you'll spread adhesive on the back; other papers are prepasted—you just soak them in water before hanging. After pasting or soaking, "book" the strips (see illustration at left).

**Hanging the wallpaper.** Place a stepladder next to the plumb line you've marked. Open the top fold of the first booked strip, overlapping the ceiling line by 2 inches. Align the strip's edge with the plumb line.

Using a smoothing brush, press the strip against the wall. Smooth out all wrinkles and air bubbles. Then release the lower portion of the strip and smooth it into place.

Roll the edges flat with a seam roller. To trim along the ceiling and baseboard, use a broad knife and a very sharp razor knife. Remove any excess adhesive with a sponge dipped in lukewarm water.

Unfold the second strip on the wall. Gently butt the second against the first, aligning the pattern along the edge. Continue around the room.

**Corners.** Because few rooms have perfectly straight corners, you will have to measure from the edge of the preceding strip to the corner; do this at three heights. Cut a strip ½ inch wider than the widest measurement. Butting this strip to the preceding one, brush it firmly into and around the corner. At the top and bottom corners, cut the overlap.

Next, measure the width of the left-over piece of wallpaper. On the adjacent wall, measure the same distance from the corner; make a plumb line at that point.

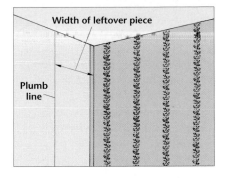

Width of leftover piece

Plumb line

Position one edge of the strip along the plumb line; the other edge will cover the ½-inch overlap. (If you are hanging vinyl wallpaper, apply a vinyl-to-vinyl adhesive on top of the overlapping edge.)

**Cutouts.** Shut off the electricity before making any cutouts. Hang the paper, then use a razor knife to make an X-shaped cut over the opening. Make sure the cuts extend to each corner. Then trim the excess paper.

## HANGING THE FIRST STRIP

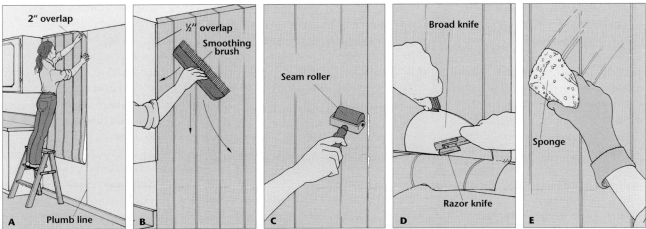

2" overlap

Plumb line

A

½" overlap

Smoothing brush

B

Seam roller

C

Broad knife

Razor knife

D

Sponge

E

**To hang wallpaper,** first open the top fold of the strip, overlap the ceiling line, and align the strip's edge with the plumb line (A); press the strip against the wall with a smoothing brush (B). Release the lower fold and smooth into place; roll the edges flat with a seam roller (C). Trim the strip along the ceiling and baseboard with a broad knife and a razor knife (D). Remove excess adhesive with a sponge dipped in lukewarm water (E).

# Painting tips

A fresh coat of paint provides the fastest way to brighten up your bathroom. Here are some guidelines to help you do a professional job.

## SELECTING TOOLS AND MATERIALS

One key to a good paint job is to choose the right materials.

**Paint.** Your basic choices are water-based or latex paint and oil-based or alkyd paint. Latex is easy to work with and cleans up with soap and water. Alkyd paint provides a durable high-gloss finish and will last longer but is trickier to apply and requires cleanup with mineral spirits.

In general, a high resin content is the mark of durable, flexible, and abrasion-resistant paint—the kind you need in a bathroom. Usually, the higher the resin content, the higher the gloss, so look for products labeled gloss or semigloss.

A good choice for bathroom cabinets and woodwork is quick-drying alkyd enamel. It has a brilliant, tile-like finish that's extremely durable.

**Tools.** Natural bristles are traditionally used to apply oil-based paints; synthetic bristles are best for latex paint. For window sashes and trim,

choose a 1½- or 2-inch angled sash brush. A 2- or 3-inch brush or paint pad is best for woodwork, doors, and cabinets. A 9-inch roller is good for painting large flat areas.

## PREPARING THE SURFACE

To prevent cracking and peeling after the paint dries, you must begin with surfaces that are smooth and clean.

It's possible to paint over wallpaper that's smooth and attached firmly to the wall. Apply a sealing primer such as pigmented shellac or a flat oil-based enamel undercoat. Let the sealer dry completely before you paint. It's often safer, though, to remove the wallpaper.

**Repair the finish.** For an old paint finish, sanding is sufficient if the surface is flaking lightly. Wash dirty areas on a wood surface before sanding.

Roughen glossy paint surfaces with sandpaper so the new paint will adhere. (Rough, bare wood also needs sanding, as do patched areas.)

When a wood finish is in poor condition, you'll have to strip it. You can use an electric paint softener or heat gun, or a commercial liquid paint remover. With either method, take off the softened paint with a broad knife or paint scraper, then

sand the surface lightly until it is clean and smooth.

Carefully inspect the surface for holes and cracks and repair them with spackling compound.

Finally, dust everything, then vacuum the floor. With an abrasive cleaner, sponge the areas to be painted, then rinse. Let washed areas dry completely for 24 hours.

**Prime the surface.** Be sure to prime any unpainted plaster or drywall. Use the primer recommended by the paint manufacturer.

## APPLYING THE PAINT

To avoid painting yourself into a corner, follow the sequence below.

**Ceiling.** If you're painting both the walls and the ceiling, begin with the ceiling. Paint the entire surface in one session. It's best to paint in 2- by 3-foot rectangles, starting in a corner and working across the shortest dimension of the room.

On the first section use a brush or special corner pad to paint a narrow strip next to the wall line and around any fixtures. Then finish the section with a roller, overlapping any brush marks. Work your way back and forth across the ceiling, painting one section at a time.

**Walls.** Mentally divide a wall into 3-foot-square sections, starting from a corner at the ceiling line and working down the wall. As with ceilings, paint the edges first with a brush or corner roller, painting along the ceiling line, corners, fixtures, and door edges. Finish each section with a roller or brush, overlapping any brush marks.

At the bottom of the walls above the floor or baseboard, and along the edges of the medicine cabinet and vanity, use a brush and a painting guide to get a neat, even edge. Overlap the brush strokes with a roller. As a final step, return to the ceiling line and again work down the walls in 3-foot sections.

## TOOLS OF THE PAINTING TRADE

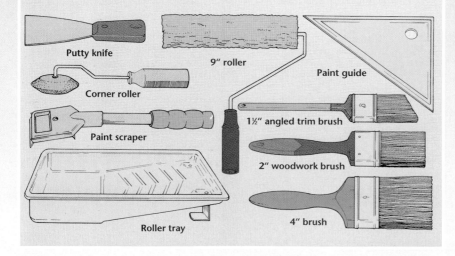

Putty knife

9" roller

Paint guide

Corner roller

Paint scraper

1½" angled trim brush

2" woodwork brush

Roller tray

4" brush

## CERAMIC TILE

Few wallcoverings have the decorative impact and durability of ceramic tile. It's a natural choice for any wall that might be splashed—water and soap film can be cleaned away in seconds.

On these pages you'll learn how to remove and install ceramic tile.

For information on various types of wall tile, see page 63. If your plans call for a ceramic tile floor, install the floor tiles before setting tiles on the wall (see page 108).

### REMOVING CERAMIC TILE

Removing wall tile set in mortar is a tough job. If possible, replace only those tiles that are damaged. If tiles are clean and smooth and the wall surface is flat, consider installing the new tiles directly over them.

If you must remove old tile, proceed with caution (see "Removing the wallcovering" on page 89). You may prefer to have a professional remove tile that is set in mortar.

If your wall tile is set on drywall, you can more easily remove it yourself. Wearing goggles and a dust mask, use a cold chisel and ball-peen hammer to chip through the tile and backing. Once you've removed small sections, insert a pry bar and pry off large sections of the tile and backing until the wall studs are exposed.

Next, inspect the exposed wall framing for any water damage, and replace framing members if necessary. Then you can install backing for your new tile or for any other wallcovering of your choice.

### INSTALLING CERAMIC TILE

Plan and prepare carefully before you install tile. First measure your bathroom and sketch your walls on graph paper. Choose and plan the placement of special trim pieces, such as bullnose, cove, and quarter-round edging tiles, as well as ceramic accessories—soap dishes, paper holders, and toothbrush holders. Your dealer can help you select trim pieces.

Once you have designed your walls and selected tile, you're ready to begin.

Described below are the steps you will need to follow to install your tile, from preparing the backing to finishing the wall. (If you're installing pregrouted tile panels, follow the manufacturer's instructions.)

Before you start, remove baseboards and window and door trim, any wall-mounted accessories and lights, and, as necessary, the toilet, bidet, and sink.

**Prepare the backing surface.** This is probably the most important step in installing wall tile successfully. Backing must be solid, flat, clean, and dry.

You can use existing drywall or even wood or tile as backing if it's in good condition. You may need to clean, smooth out, or prime these surfaces before you're ready for new tile; ask your tile dealer for recommendations.

You may opt for new drywall backing. But for wet areas, it's safest to install cement backer board or the gypsum-based variety, available in 3-foot widths and various lengths. Standard panel thickness for new installations is ½ inch. Though it's not strictly necessary, a waterproof membrane behind the backer board helps ensure a watertight wall.

**Cut cement backer board.** Measure and cut each panel carefully so that the edge will be placed in the center of a stud. To cut the panels, mark the cutting line directly on the cement board. Using a straightedge as a guide, score a line in the board with a utility knife. To break the core, place the edges of a stack of 2 by 4s under the cut and press down on the panel. (See page 98 for drawings of a similar method of cutting drywall.)

To complete the cut, lift up the panel and use a utility knife to cut through the mesh backing.

**Make cutouts.** Measure the center of any holes for pipes and mark them on the board. To start the hole, tap a dent in the center with an awl. Then drill through the dent with a carbide-tip bit. Make the hole slightly larger than necessary, to make the installation a little easier. Or start the hole with a small-diameter masonry bit and then use a saber saw to cut out the hole.

**Install the cement board.** Cement board is rigid, unlike drywall, and will not bend to conform to a frame. Make sure your frame is even. Fasten panels to wall studs with 1½-inch galvanized roofing nails. Cover all edge and corner joints with fiberglass drywall tape. You don't need to use drywall compound.

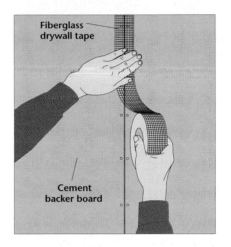

**Tiles and adhesive.** For setting tiles on bathroom walls, choose either thinset (cement-base) or epoxy adhesive. Thinset adhesive, when mixed with a latex additive, is adequate for most jobs; epoxy is slightly more difficult to work with and more expensive. The same distinctions apply to cement-base and epoxy grouts. Read the labels and consult your tile dealer to determine which adhesive and grout are best for your situation.

Once your backing is prepared, you are ready to mark the working lines.

**Mark working lines.** Accurate horizontal and vertical working lines help you keep tiles properly aligned so that your finished wall will look level and even. The horizontal working line should be near the bottom of the wall, because tiling up a wall is easier than tiling down.

If you're tiling around a tub, establish working lines there first. This way, you can plan for a row of full (uncut) tiles just above the tub, at the bather's eye level. This works best if the tub is level to within ⅛ inch. Locate the high point of the tub lip with your level, then measure up one tile width plus ⅛ inch. Mark a level line on the wall through this point; then extend the line carefully across all adjoining walls. This will give you a bottom row of full tiles around the tub. (You can fill in any small gaps below them with caulking later.)

If your tub is not level to within ⅛ inch, locate the horizontal working line from the low point of the tub lip, and follow the above method. You'll have to cut the bottom row of tiles to fit.

Then, on walls adjoining the tub, establish a line close to the floor. Start at the working line you extend from the tub wall and measure down a full number of tiles, including grout joints. Leave a space at least one full tile high above the floor. Mark the horizontal working line for this wall through this point with a straightedge and level (see illustrations below).

To establish a line on a wall not adjoining a tub, find the lowest point by setting a level on the floor at various locations against the walls to be tiled. At the lowest point, place a tile against the wall and mark its top edge on the wall. If you're installing a cove base, set a cove tile on the floor and a wall tile above it (allow for the grout joint); then mark the top of the wall tile. Using a level and straightedge, draw a horizontal line through the mark across the wall. Extend this line onto the other walls that are to be tiled.

After marking your horizontal working lines, nail battens (1- by 2-inch wood strips) all along the walls,

## PATTERN FOR SETTING TILE

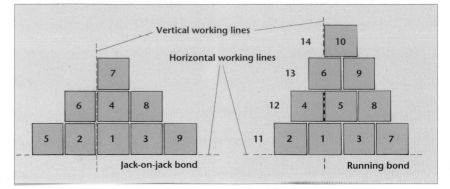

with their top edges on the lines. These will be your horizontal guides.

To establish a vertical working line, locate the midpoint of a wall and mark it on the horizontal working line. Starting at this point, set up a row of loose tiles along the wall on the batten to see how they will fit at the ends of the wall.

If you end up with less than half a tile on both ends, move your mark one-half a tile to the right or left to avoid ending the rows with narrow pieces. Then extend this vertical working line through your mark and up the wall with a straightedge and level (see illustration below).

If you don't plan to tile to the ceiling line, mark the point where the highest tile will be set. Using a level, draw a horizontal line through this point across the wall.

Finally, be sure to mark locations of ceramic towel bars, soap dishes, and other accessories.

**Set the tile.** First, prepare the tile adhesive according to the manufacturer's directions. (Be sure to keep your working area well ventilated.)

To determine how large an area to cover at one time, consult the adhesive container label for the open time—the length of time you have to work with the adhesive after spreading. Comb through the adhesive with a notched trowel to form ridges.

When you set the tiles, place each one with a slight twist—don't slide it. Keep spacing for grout joints uniform. Some tiles have small ceramic spacing lugs molded onto their edges; if your tiles don't have them, drive 6-penny finishing nails into the drywall to act as temporary spacing guides (see illustration page 105, top left).

The way you will begin setting tiles depends on which bond you use—jack-on-jack (with joints lined up) or running bond (with staggered joints).

For a jack-on-jack bond, set the first tile on the batten so that one side is aligned exactly with the vertical working line. Set additional tiles as shown in the illustration above, forming a pyramid pattern. For a running bond, center the first tile directly on the vertical working line, then follow the pyramid pattern illustrated above as you set the tile.

With either type of bond, continue setting tiles upward and toward the ends of the walls in the pattern illustrated above. After laying several tiles, set

## WORKING LINES FOR TILE

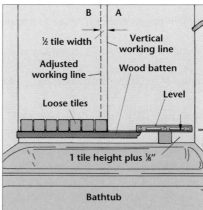

**Extend horizontal working line** around tub to adjoining walls, then measure to floor. Extend the line along the adjoining walls.

**To establish vertical working line,** locate the midpoint of the wall (A), then adjust (B) according to the size of the end tiles.

them into the adhesive by sliding a carpet-wrapped piece of plywood across the tiles as you tap it gently with a hammer.

Cut tiles to fit at the end of each horizontal row and at the top near the ceiling. (Use a rented tile cutter to cut straight pieces; use nippers to cut out irregular shapes.) For the top row of any installation that doesn't reach all the way to the ceiling, set a row of bullnose or cap tiles.

When you come to a wall where there are electrical outlets or switches, turn off the power to them. Remove the cover plates, if installed, and pull the outlets and switches from their boxes, but don't disconnect them. Cut and fit tiles around the boxes, then re-mount the outlets and switches.

On inside corners, butt the tiles together. On outside corners, set one column of bullnose tiles to cover the unfinished edges of the tiles on each adjoining wall.

### INSTALLING WALL TILE

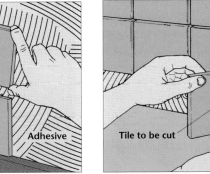

**To space wall tiles** not molded with spacing lugs, place 6-penny finishing nails between the tiles.

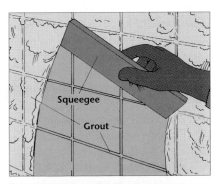

**Spread grout on the tile,** forcing it into the joints with a float or squeegee until they are full. Remove the excess grout.

Around windows, finish off the sides and sills with bullnose tiles cut to fit the space.

Install ceramic accessories such as soap dishes in spaces you left open when tiling. Tape the accessories in place while the adhesive sets.

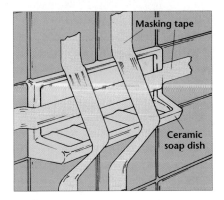

Now check your work. If anything is out of alignment, wiggle it into po-sition before the adhesive sets. Clean adhesive from the face of tiles and accessories, and from joint spaces.

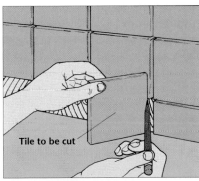

**To set a bottom row of tiles,** remove batten on working line, mark tile, and cut. Set in adhesive as for other tiles.

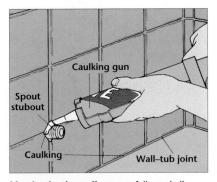

**Use bathtub caulk** to carefully seal all the openings between the fixtures or the pipes and the tile.

When the adhesive has set, care-fully remove the battens. Then twist the nail spacers as you pull them out from the wall.

Spread adhesive at the bottom of the wall where the battens were and set the remaining tiles, cutting them to fit as needed.

**Grout the tile.** Before grouting, allow the adhesive to set properly—usually you must allow 16 hours for epoxy-base adhesive and 48 hours for the cement-base type.

Remove any excess adhesive from the tile joints. Then mix the grout recommended for your tile and spread it on the surface of the tile with a rubber-faced float or a squeegee, forcing it into the tile joints until they're completely filled. Scrape off excess grout from the tile, working diagonally across the sur-face of the tiles.

Wipe the tiles with a wet grout sponge to remove any remaining grout. Rinse and wring out the sponge frequently, wiping until the grout joints are smooth and level with the tile surface. When the tiles are as clean as you can get them, let the grout dry until a haze appears over the surface. Then polish the haze off the tiles with a soft cloth. Finish (tool) the joints with the end of a toothbrush handle.

**Seal tile and grout.** Installations with unglazed tile or with cement-based grout need to be protected by a grout and tile sealer. Most sealers for use with bathroom tiles have a silicone base.

Be sure to follow the manufactur-er's instructions for applying these sealers. Both tiles and grout should be dry. On new tile, you must wait at least two weeks to give the grout a chance to cure completely. Apply a moderate amount of sealer, and wipe off any excess to prevent the sealer from discoloring the tile.

Finally, use caulking to seal all openings or gaps between the pipes or fixtures and the tile. Then replace all trim, accessories, and fixtures.

Two requirements for bathroom floors are moisture resistance and durability. Resilient flooring and ceramic tile are ideal choices on both counts. If you're planning a complete remodeling of your bathroom, this is a good time to put in ceramic tile, since it's ideally installed with cabinets, doors, and fixtures removed from the room. If you're replacing only the floor, resilient flooring is a good choice; it can be installed around most fixtures and cabinets.

The information in this section assumes that your floor is supported by a standard subfloor, with joists or beams below it (see illustration on page 67). If your home is built on a concrete slab and your flooring will be installed over it, you need to make sure that the slab is dry, level, and clean before you begin any work.

## RESILIENT SHEET FLOORING

Resilient sheet flooring is available with smooth or textured surfaces, in plain colors or in patterns. Though a few types are available in widths up to 12 feet, most sheet flooring is only 6 feet wide, so seams may be necessary.

**Plan the new floor.** Take exact measurements of the floor and make a scale drawing on graph paper. If your room is very irregular, you may want to make a full-size paper pattern of the floor rather than the scale drawing.

**Prepare the subfloor.** Both wood and old resilient flooring make acceptable bases for new resilient sheets, provided their surfaces are completely smooth and level. Old resilient flooring must be solid, not cushioned, and firmly bonded to the subfloor. Uneven wood floors may need a rough sanding. Both types of existing floors must be thoroughly cleaned, and any loose pieces must be secured.

If the old floor is cushioned or in poor condition, it should be removed

down to the subfloor if possible. If the old flooring is impossible to remove without damaging the subfloor, or if the subfloor is in poor condition, cover the old flooring with ¼-inch underlayment-grade plywood or untempered hardboard. (If there are signs of water damage or insect infestation, consult a professional.)

**Cut the flooring.** The most critical step in laying sheet flooring is making the first rough cuts accurately. You may ask your flooring dealer to make these first cuts for you; if so, you'll need to supply a floor plan.

To cut the flooring to size yourself, unroll the material in a large room. Transfer the floor plan directly onto the new flooring, using chalk or a water-soluble felt-tip pen, a carpenter's square, and a straightedge.

If your flooring will have a seam, be sure to allow for overlap or for matching the pattern (if any) on adjoining sheets. If your flooring has simulated grout or mortar joints, plan to cut the seam along the midpoint of a joint.

Using a linoleum or utility knife, cut the flooring so it's roughly about 3 inches larger on all sides (this excess will be trimmed away after the flooring has been put in place).

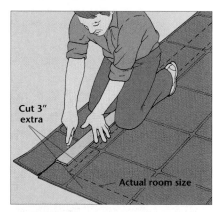

Cut 3" extra

Actual room size

If a seam is necessary, cut and install the piece of flooring that requires the most intricate fitting first; then cut and install the second sheet.

**Install the flooring.** Following are instructions for laying resilient sheet

flooring using adhesive. Some types of sheet flooring can be laid without adhesive. In this case, you simply roll out the flooring and shift it until it's in the proper position, then apply adhesive around the edges or staple the edges in place. If you are considering this easy installation method, check with your flooring dealer to be sure the material you have selected does not require adhesive on the entire back.

If you're installing a single piece of flooring, you can spread adhesive over the entire subfloor at once or spread adhesive in steps as the flooring is unrolled. First check the adhesive's open time—that is, the time you have to work with the adhesive while it is still tacky. Be sure to follow the directions of the adhesive manufacturer.

If the entire floor has been covered with adhesive, slowly roll the flooring out across the floor, taking care to set the flooring firmly into the adhesive as you go. If you're working a section at a time, spread adhesive and unroll the flooring as you go.

If you are installing flooring with seams, spread the adhesive on the subflooring as directed by the adhesive manufacturer, but stop 8 or 9 inches from the seam. Then position the first sheet on the floor.

Next, position the second sheet of flooring carefully so that it overlaps the first sheet by at least 2 inches; make sure the design is perfectly aligned. Then roll up the flooring and spread adhesive over the remainder of the floor, stopping 8 or 9 inches from the edge of the first sheet of flooring. Now reposition the second sheet of flooring, starting at the seam. Again, take care to align the design perfectly. Then roll the flooring out, carefully setting it into the adhesive.

When the flooring is in position, trim away the excess flooring at each end of the seam in a half-moon shape so the ends butt against the wall.

Using a steel straightedge and a sharp utility knife, make a straight cut (about ½ or ⅝ inch from the edge

## TRIMMING RESILIENT SHEETS

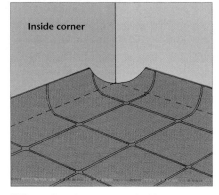

**Where flooring turns** an inside corner, cut the excess with diagonal cuts.

**At an outside corner,** cut straight down to the point where the wall and floor meet.

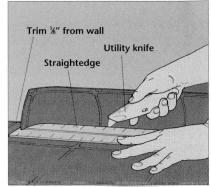

**Trim flooring,** leaving a ⅛" gap between the edge and the wall.

of the top sheet) down through both sheets. Then lift up the flooring on either side of the seam, remove the two overlap strips, and spread adhesive on the subfloor under the seam.

Use the recommended solvent to clean adhesive from around the seam. When the seam is dry and clean, use the recommended seam sealer to fuse the two pieces.

**Trim to fit.** When the flooring has been positioned, you'll need to make a series of relief cuts at all corners so the flooring will lie flat (see above).

At outside corners, start at the top of the excess flooring and cut straight down to the point where the wall and floor meet. At inside corners, cut the excess flooring away a little at a time until it lies flat.

To remove the excess flooring along a wall, press the flooring into a right angle where the floor and wall join, using an 18- to 24-inch-long piece of 2 by 4. Then lay a heavy metal straightedge along the wall and trim the flooring with a utility knife, leaving a gap of about ⅛ inch between the edge of the flooring and the wall to allow the material to expand without buckling.

## RESILIENT TILE FLOORING

Resilient tiles come in 12-inch squares. Other sizes and shapes are available by special order.

To determine the amount of tile you will need, first find the area of the floor,

subtracting for any large protrusions. Add 5 percent so you'll have extra tiles for cutting and later repairs. If your design uses more than one color, estimate how many tiles of each color you will need by coloring in your floor plan with colored pencils.

**Place the tiles.** Laying resilient tiles involves three steps: marking the working lines, spreading the adhesive (unless you are using self-stick tiles), and placing the tiles. These steps are similar to those for ceramic tile (for details, see page 108). But unlike ceramic tiles, resilient tiles are laid tightly against each other and, because they are made with machine precision, they must be laid out in perfectly straight lines.

Once a tile is in position, press it firmly in place. Lay half a dozen or so, setting them by going over them with a

## TRIMMING RESILIENT TILES

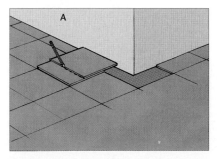

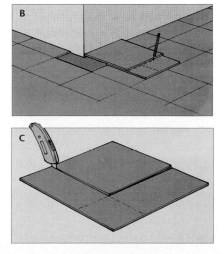

**To lay out a border tile,** first place a loose tile on top of the last full tile nearest the wall; then place a second tile over the first, butting it against the wall, and mark the first tile for cutting (A). This same technique can be used to mark L-shaped tiles for outside corners (B). Score tiles with a utility knife (C).

rolling pin. If you are using self-stick tiles, take extra care to position them exactly before you press them into place, because they are hard to remove once they are fixed to the floor. Also note the arrows on the back of self-stick tiles—lay the tiles with all the arrows going the same way.

**Cut the tile.** To cut tiles, score them along the mark with a utility knife; then snap the tile along the line. For intricate cuts, use heavy scissors or tin snips. (The tiles will cut more easily if warmed first in sunlight or over a furnace vent.)

To mark border and corner tiles for cutting, position a loose tile exactly over one of the tiles in the last row closest to the wall (see below). Place another loose tile on top of the first, butting it against the wall. Using this tile as a guide, mark the tile beneath for cutting.

Installing a new floor of ceramic tile can be a very satisfying do-it-yourself project. New, easy-to-install tiles and improved adhesives and grouts make it possible for a careful, patient do-it-yourselfer to create a ceramic tile floor of professional quality.

Because it's usually possible to use existing ceramic tile as a subfloor (see "Prepare the subfloor," below), this section covers installation only—not removal. It's not easy to remove an old tile floor, particularly if the tiles were laid in mortar. So if removal of the tiles is necessary, it is a good idea to consult a professional.

Installing a ceramic tile floor is essentially a three-step operation: you lay evenly spaced tiles in a bed of adhesive atop a properly prepared subfloor, fill the joint spaces between tiles with grout, and seal the floor for durability and easy cleaning. In this section you'll find basic instructions for laying tile flooring; if you need more detailed information, turn to a contractor or your tile supplier.

**Prepare the subfloor.** Floors covered with ceramic tile, masonry, wood, and resilient flooring (except the cushion type) can be successfully covered with ceramic tile—provided the old floor is well bonded, level, clean, and dry.

If the existing flooring is in poor condition, you'll need to repair, cover, or remove it before you can proceed. Fasten loose ceramic, masonry, or resilient flooring with adhesive; nail down loose wood flooring; fill gouges in resilient flooring; and sand wood floors smooth.

If the existing flooring is so badly damaged that it's beyond repair—or if there is a cushioned resilient flooring in place—it will need to be removed down to the subfloor, if possible. If it is impossible to remove the old flooring without damaging the subfloor underneath, or if the subfloor is in very poor condition, you can cover the existing flooring with either a sheet of ⅜-inch-thick underlayment-grade plywood or untempered hardboard.

Ask your tile dealer to recommend the best adhesive for your new tile floor, because the type of adhesive depends on the type of flooring you'll be covering. Follow your tile dealer's instructions for how to prepare the subfloor, and be sure to check the directions on the adhesive container for additional information.

**Establish working lines.** The key to laying straight rows of tile is to first establish very accurate working lines. Following are instructions for laying out working lines from the center of the room. This method makes it easy to keep rows even and is the best method to use if the room is out of square or if you've chosen a tile with a definite pattern or design.

First locate the center point on each of two opposite walls and snap a chalk line on the floor between the two points. Then find the centers of the other two walls and stretch your chalk line at right angles to the first line; snap the line only after you've used a carpenter's square to determine that the two lines cross at a precise right angle. If they don't, adjust the lines until they do.

Make a dry run before you actually set the tiles in adhesive. Lay one row of tiles along each working line, from the center of the room to each of two adjoining walls. Make sure you allow proper spacing for grout joints. Adjust your working lines as necessary to avoid very narrow border tiles.

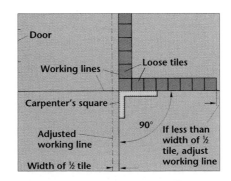

If you are working over a wood subfloor, temporarily nail batten boards along the two working lines that outline the quarter of the room

farthest from the door; the battens will provide a rigid guide for the first row of tiles. (If you are working over a masonry subfloor, you'll have to use the chalk lines as your guides.) You'll set tiles using the sequence shown below, completing the floor quarter by quarter. Work on the quarter by the doorway last.

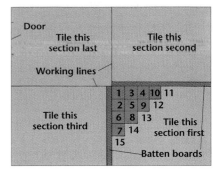

**Set the tiles.** Using a notched trowel, start spreading adhesive. Cover about a square yard at first, or the size area you can comfortably tile before the adhesive begins to set.

Using a gentle twisting motion, place the first tile in the corner formed by the two battens or chalk lines. With the same motion, place a second tile alongside the first. Continue laying the tiles, following the sequence illustrated above. Use molded plastic spacers to establish the proper width for the grout joints.

As the tiles are laid, set a piece of carpet-wrapped wood over them and gently tap the wood with a rubber mallet or hammer to "beat in" the tiles. Keep checking with a carpenter's square or straightedge to make sure each row is straight. Wiggle any stray tiles back into position.

To fit border tiles, measure each space carefully, subtract the width of two grout joints, and mark each tile for any necessary cuts.

When you have tiled the first quarter of the floor, remove the batten boards and work on the next quarter. After all the tiles are placed, remove the spacers and clean the tile surface so it's completely free of adhesive.

Grout and seal the tile following the instructions for wall tile on page 105.

In many homes, the need for bathroom storage has increased as people have collected a great number of personal belongings—bulky electric grooming appliances, children's bath toys, and cleaning supplies. For many families, a medicine cabinet simply doesn't provide enough space.

This section will show you how you can gain space by installing a floor-mounted vanity cabinet, then topping it with countertops of plastic laminate or ceramic tile.

## VANITY CABINETS

You can select a vanity cabinet to complement almost any style of bathroom. The vanity may be fitted with various types of countertops and sinks (see pages 54–56).

Regardless of what countertop and sink you prefer, the methods for removing and installing a prefabricated vanity cabinet in your bathroom are the same.

If a vanity cabinet taller than standard height is more comfortable, add a frame of suitable height underneath the bottom before installing the cabinet.

### REMOVING A VANITY CABINET

To remove a plumbed vanity, you will need to disconnect the plumbing and remove the sink and countertop (see pages 82–83).

Pry away any vinyl wall base, floor covering, or molding from the side or kickspace below the base cabinet.

Old vanity cabinets are usually attached to wall studs with screws or nails through nailing strips at the back of each unit. Sometimes they're also fastened to the floor. Screws are easy to remove unless they're old and stripped. To remove nails, you may need to pry the cabinet away from the wall or floor with a pry bar. To prevent damage, use a wood scrap between the pry bar and the wall or floor. For a vanity with a solid back, you may have to first shut off the water at the main valve and

remove the sink shutoff valves to pull the vanity away from the wall.

### INSTALLING A VANITY CABINET

Before you begin, remove any moldings, baseboard or wall base that might interfere. From the floor, measure up 34½ inches—the height of a standard vanity cabinet. Take several measurements and use the highest mark for your reference point. Then draw a level line through this mark and across the wall.

If the vanity has a solid back, you must measure, mark, and cut the holes for the drain and water supply pipes, using a keyhole or saber saw.

For both solid and open-back vanities, locate and mark all wall studs (see page 68) in the wall above where the vanity will be installed. Move the vanity into place.

Level the top of the vanity from side to side and front to back, shimming between the vanity and floor as needed. Both shims and irregularities in the floor can be hidden by baseboard trim.

Some cabinets are designed with "scribing strips" along the sides. Other manufacturers offer decorative panels to "finish" the end of a cabinet run. Both designs include extra material you can shave down to achieve a perfect fit between the cabinet and an irregular wall.

To scribe a cabinet, first position it; then place a length of masking tape down the side to be scribed. Setting the points of a compass with pencil to the widest gap between the scribing strip and the wall, run the compass pivot down the wall next to the strip, as illustrated below. The wall's irregularities will be marked on the tape. Remove the vanity from the wall and use a block plane, file, or power belt sander to trim the scribing strip to the line. Then reinstall the cabinet.

If your cabinet doesn't have scribing strips, you can cover any large irregularities between the wall and cabinet with decorative molding. Scribe the molding as required.

Once the cabinet is aligned with your reference marks on the wall, extend the stud location marks down to the hanger strip on the back of the vanity. Drill pilot holes through the strip into the wall studs, and secure the vanity to the studs with wood screws or drywall screws. If the wall studs are not accessible, you can fasten the vanity with wall anchors.

Once the vanity cabinet is securely in place, install the countertop and sink, then connect the water supply lines, the trap, and the pop-up drain (see pages 83–85).

### INSTALLING A VANITY CABINET

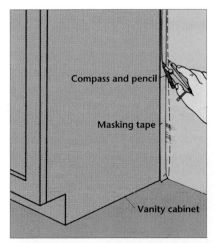

**Scribe and trim** sides of the vanity to make a snug fit when the wall is out of plumb or is uneven.

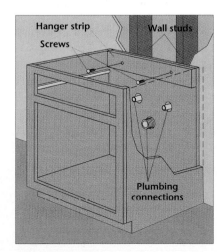

**Secure the vanity cabinet** to the studs by screwing through the hanger strip across the back. Drill pilot holes first.

## POST-FORMED LAMINATE COUNTERTOP

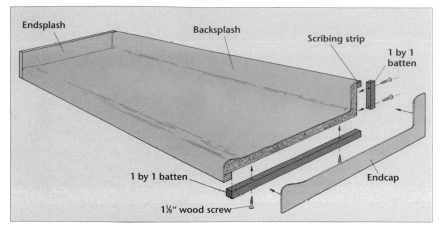

Endsplash

Backsplash

Scribing strip

1 by 1 batten

1 by 1 batten

1⅛" wood screw

Endcap

## COUNTERTOPS

Plastic laminate and tile are two very popular materials for countertops. Both are durable, water resistant, and straightforward to install.

### INSTALLING A PLASTIC LAMINATE COUNTERTOP

Laminate countertops are divided into two different types: post-formed and custom. Post-formed countertops are premolded one-piece tops, from curved backsplash to bullnose front. The term "custom" means that you apply the laminate of your choice over a core material.

**Post-formed countertop.** Since post-formed countertops come only in standard sizes, you'll normally need to buy one slightly larger than

you need and cut it to length. To cut the countertop with a handsaw or table saw, mark the cut line on the face. Mark the back if you're using a circular saw or saber saw. Use a piece of masking tape to protect the cutting line against chipping (you will likely have to redraw the line, this time on the tape). Smooth the edge of the cut with a file or sandpaper. Plan to cover that end with an endsplash or endcap (a preshaped strip of matching laminate).

Endsplashes are screwed into the edge of the countertop or into "built-down" wood battens attached to the edge, as shown above. Endcaps are glued to an open end of the counter with contact cement or, in some cases, pressed into place with a hot iron.

Countertops, like cabinets, rarely fit uniformly against walls. Usually, the back edge of a post-formed countertop

comes with a scribing strip that can be trimmed to follow the exact contours of the wall. To use the scribing strip, follow the instructions for scribing cabinets on page 109.

Now fasten the countertop to the cabinets by placing screws from below through the cabinet corner gussets or top frame and through any shims or wood blocks. Use wood screws that are just long enough to penetrate ½ inch into the countertop core. Then run a bead of silicone sealant along all the exposed seams between the countertop and the walls.

**Custom countertop.** To build your own laminate countertop, you will need to choose the laminate (1/16-inch thickness is the standard) and cut the core material to size from a piece of ¾-inch plywood or high-density particleboard.

First, build down the edges of the core with 1 by 3 battens (see the illustration below). Then you are ready to laminate the countertop. Work on sides and front strips first and then the top surface.

Next, measure each surface to be laminated, adding at least ¼ inch to all dimensions as a margin for error. Mark the cutting line. Score the line with a sharp utility knife; then cut with a fine-toothed saw (face up with a handsaw or table saw, face down with a circular saw or saber saw).

Apply contact cement to both the laminate back and the core surface to be joined, and allow the cement to dry for 20 to 30 minutes. Carefully check alignment before joining the two; once joined, the laminate cannot be moved. Press the laminate into place, using a roller or a rolling pin to ensure even contact.

Now use a block plane to trim the laminate flush with the edges of the core; then dress it with a file. Or trim with an electric router equipped with a laminate-trimming bit.

The backsplashes and endsplashes should be cut from the same core material as the main countertop, then butt joined to the countertop with a sealant and wood screws.

## CUSTOM LAMINATE COUNTERTOP

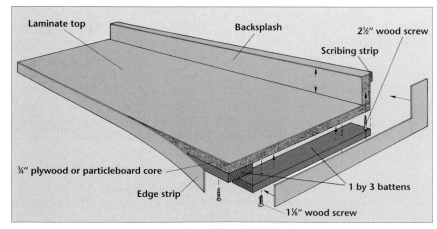

Laminate top

Backsplash

2½" wood screw

Scribing strip

¾" plywood or particleboard core

Edge strip

1 by 3 battens

1⅛" wood screw

## INSTALLING A CERAMIC TILE COUNTERTOP

Wall tiles, lighter and thinner than floor tiles, are a good choice for bathroom countertops and backsplashes. Standard sizes range from 3 inches by 3 inches to $4\frac{1}{2}$ inches by $8\frac{1}{2}$ inches, with thicknesses varying from $\frac{1}{4}$ inch to $\frac{3}{8}$ inch. Another choice, mosaic tiles (see page 63), makes your job easier, especially in backsplash areas.

**Prepare the base.** Before laying tile, remove any old countertops; then install $\frac{3}{4}$-inch exterior plywood cut flush with the cabinet top, screwing it to the cabinet frame from below. For moisture resistance, add a waterproof membrane, followed by a layer of cement backer board on top.

Surfaces may need to be primed or sealed before tile is applied. To determine the best base and preparation for your job, read the information on the adhesive container or ask your tile supplier for advice.

**Plan the layout.** Before you start laying tile, you must decide how you want to trim the countertop edge and the sink. For trimming ideas, see the illustration below.

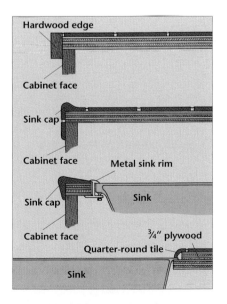

If you decide to trim the tiles with wood, seal the wood and attach it to the cabinet face with finishing nails. When it's in place, the wood strip's top

## HOW TO SET COUNTERTOP TILES

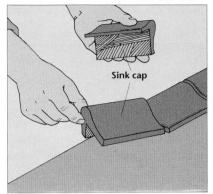

**First, butter the backs** of the edge tiles with adhesive, then set them in place, starting from the center line.

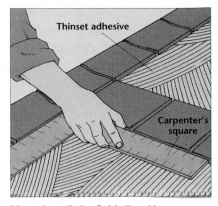

**Next, install the field tiles.** Use a carpenter's square to keep the tiles perpendicular to the edge trim.

edge should be positioned at the same height as the finished tile. A recessed or undermounted sink, often used with tile countertops, is also installed at this time (see page 85).

On the front edge of the plywood base, locate and mark the point where the center of the sink or midpoint of a blank countertop will be. Lay the edge tiles out on the countertop, starting from your mark. Some tiles have small ceramic lugs molded onto their edges to keep the spacing equal; if your tiles don't, you can use plastic spacers that are available from your tile supplier.

Carefully position the rest of the "field" tiles on the countertop. Looking at the layout, make any necessary adjustments to eliminate narrow cuts or difficult fits.

If the countertop will have a backsplash or will turn a corner, be sure to figure the necessary cove or corner tiles into your layout.

Mark reference points of your layout on the plywood base to help you re-create it later; then remove the tile.

**Set the tiles.** Set all the trim tiles before spreading adhesive for the field tiles. Thin-set adhesive, mixed with latex additive, is water resistant and easy to use.

Butter the back of each front-edge tile and press it into place, aligning it with the reference marks on the plywood. If your edge trim consists of two rows of tiles, set the vertical piece first.

Next, butter any back cove tiles and set them against the wall. If you have installed a recessed sink, lay the sink trim next. Be sure to caulk between the sink and the base before setting the trim. If you are using quarter-round trim, you can either miter the corners or use special corner pieces available with some patterns.

Spread adhesive over a section of the countertop. Begin laying the field tiles, working from front to back (see illustrations above). Cut the tiles to fit as necessary. As you lay tiles, check the alignment frequently with a straight-edge or carpenter's square.

To set the tiles and level their faces, slide a 1-foot-square scrap of cloth-covered plywood over them and tap the plywood with a hammer.

Unless you are tiling all the way up to an overhead cabinet or window sill, use bullnose tiles for the last row. If a wall contains electrical switches or plug-in outlets, you can cut tiles in two and use tile nippers to nip out a hole.

**Apply the grout.** Remove any spacers and clean the tile surface and the grout joints until they are completely free of any adhesive. Allow thinset adhesive to set for 24 hours before grouting the joints. For information on grouting tools and techniques, see page 105.

After grouting the tiles, wait at least two weeks for the grout to cure; then you can apply the sealer recommended by your tile dealer.

# Index   Boldface numbers *refer to color photographs.*